for

ion

Studies

THE

EMERGING

INTERNET

1998

Annual Review of the
Institute for Information Studies

A Joint Program of Nortel
and The Aspen Institute

The Institute for Information Studies was established in 1987 by Nortel and The Aspen Institute, an international center for the study of leadership and public policy and their impact on corporations, individuals, communities, and society in general. Each year the IIS publishes an *Annual Review,* which is a collection of commissioned papers that provide a variety of perspectives on a particular topic relating to the impact of communications and information technology.

The *Annual Review* is prepared under the general editorial direction of Charles M. Firestone, Program Director, Institute for Information Studies, and Director, Communications and Society Program, The Aspen Institute.

 CONTENTS

INTRODUCTION

In the 1960s, one of the largest research projects funded by the U.S. Department of Defense's Advanced Research Projects Agency was Project MAC, a computer-related research program at MIT. For three summers—in 1965, 1966, and 1967—ARPA's Information Processing Techniques office invited one graduate student from Project MAC to work as a summer intern. In 1967, I was that intern, and I remained affiliated with ARPA/IPT for several years thereafter.

As has been widely—and accurately—reported over the years, the objective of one of ARPA/IPT's major projects was to develop a reliable (packet-switched) network, one that could survive a Soviet attack. A secondary objective was to develop a method of sharing computational power among geographically dispersed computers. I have always been a little bemused at the public discussions of these objectives in later years, because so much emphasis has been placed on the military basis for the project. While these defense-related objectives were indeed the project's stated goals, to overemphasize them is to ignore their context. The fact is that the Department of Defense was a primary, if not *the* primary, source of funding for public computer research at that time, so—for budgetary purposes—there was always an incentive for characterizing research projects in DoD terms. But there was certainly nothing of the urgency of a Manhattan Project in the day-to-day work environment. One simply saw computer scientists working on interesting computer and communications research problems.

As one who was "present at the creation"—albeit as a minor contributor—I can absolutely say that none of us knew then what was being created. No one was predicting that the ARPAnet, as the project came to be known, would be the precursor of that "network of networks" that we know today as the Internet. How many other endeavors in human history have started out as one (presumably well-understood) thing, only to be transformed into something else so significant, and so much greater than the vision of its original planners? Even those parts of the Internet that were already understood in those early days, such as e-mail (Project MAC had a primitive e-mail system), have evolved into something with unforeseen consequences and global implications. Some thirty years later, it is interesting that we are still trying to define and understand the implications of "the emerging Internet," often said to be "in its infancy." This thirty-year-old child has already radically altered significant aspects of human behavior and contributed greatly to the expansion and distribution of human knowledge.

* * *

In the summer of 1996, the Institute for Information Studies, a joint project of The Aspen Institute and Nortel, sponsored a conference on the future of the Internet. That meeting produced *The Internet as Paradigm*, a collection of articles examining the implications of the Internet as "an emergent paradigm, one whose lineaments are neither fully realized nor defined, but that by virtue of its obvious imaginative power characterizes and reshapes all it touches."[1] That imaginative power fueled a second Internet conference, held in the summer of 1997. This volume, *The Emerging Internet*, is the product of that meeting.

As someone fortunate enough to have been invited both times, I found myself comparing the two conferences. In just the single intervening year, the Internet had evolved from a somewhat esoteric phenomenon to mainstream reality, and the focus of the conversation had changed from the communications revolution to the societal revolution. But common to both conferences were the intense conversations in which the participants shared their understandings of the Internet, its current impact, and its possible futures. And common to both experiences was my fascinated sense that the ongoing quest to understand this "infant" technology is itself a quest to understand the emerging nature of global society within this new context: Every subject related to the Internet is related to every subject of the human experience.

Among the subjects arising in the second conference were the impact of the Internet on community, education, electronic commerce, international development, and democracy, as well as the impact *on* the Internet of national governments' struggles to retain sovereignty in the face of the Internet's insistently global nature. These subjects and their interconnections inform the papers commissioned for this volume; each chapter herein is provocative not only for its own focused content and perspective, but for the tantalizing hints of other, related ideas that the author(s) might have explored, given space enough and time. I confess my admiration for the authors of these papers, who have endeavored mightily to make these large themes digestible. I find myself facing the same challenge here in this introduction. What I shall do is begin with a broad discussion of the Internet—extrapolating some common themes of my own—and then present synopses of the book's chapters.

SOME COMMON THEMES

One of the greatest challenges surrounding any discussion of the Internet is understanding what the Internet actually *is*. Certainly, much has already been written on this subject—last year's volume is an admirable example. But the Internet is not just another aspect of the rapidly evolving computer and communications revolution, nor is it only a metaphor for something more significant. Rather, the Internet *is itself* something more significant. The challenge here is to understand what that might be—chastened by an awareness that the future seldom expresses itself as a linear extrapolation of the past. Six aspects of the Internet stand out for me:

The Internet and Qualitative Change

The Internet represents a qualitative change in computing and communications that is bringing about a qualitative change in society. A car is not a faster stagecoach, and an airplane is not a faster car. Somewhere in the transition to greater speed (a quantitative change) there also occurs a transformation in the essence of the medium itself (a change in quality). Much of the contemporary discussion surrounding the Internet limits its vision to what the Internet is or is not in today's terms. Yet, it is precisely the Internet's ability to define the terms of tomorrow—even if we don't yet know what they are—that makes the Internet so significant. We know now what we didn't know thirty years ago—that we are in the presence of a truly transformational medium—even if we still don't know where it is taking us.

This shared sense of accelerating societal transformation is the underlying theme of both the separately authored chapters in this volume and the growing global debate on the implications of the thing we call the Internet. All the other "common themes" I list below have this theme as their basic premise: Something very profound is happening. The issue is no longer faster networks, more interconnected computers or people, or greater access to information. The issue is that we are witnessing a fundamental change in selected aspects of our society, and we are not quite sure what those changes are, or where they are taking us.

People are most comfortable with change that occurs gradually, change that occurs without demanding our conscious awareness and so grants us the time to absorb its impact. This is not the kind of change that we have witnessed with the rapid advances in computing and communications that have brought about the Internet, and it is not the kind of change that we are now witnessing with the Internet itself. Its first thirty years notwithstanding, the Internet is evolving at a faster speed than any other change in the history of humankind. The popular as well as the trade press are devoting rapt attention to the increasing momentum of the Internet, recording its advances and speculating on its implications. Because no one can know where all this will lead, however, perhaps the most that we can attempt is to cultivate awareness of the changes as they occur, and to witness the evolution of our destiny.

The Internet's New Capabilities

The Internet creates new capabilities with no real counterpart in physical space. A simple technological example of this qualitative change is mentioned by Jeffrey Abramson in his chapter on the Internet and community—"Instant Messaging," a service offered by America Online, Inc., and recently licensed to Netscape Communications Corporation.[2]

Consider what Instant Messaging *is*: When you call a person on the telephone, you do not know whether the person will be at the called location to answer. If you leave a voice message, you do not know when or if the person will receive it. Even when you call a person who has a portable telephone, you cannot be certain that the person will be available at the moment of the call; the same holds for pagers. And e-mail brings its own uncertainties. But Instant Messaging works differently.

When the Instant Message service is activated, a message on your computer alerts you whenever someone at the e-mail address(es) you specify logs onto the AOL network or the Internet (using software from AOL or one of the licensees). If you want, you can then send that person an Instant Message, which will immediately appear on his or her computer screen.

To get some idea of the enormity of this capability of cyberspace, consider that in the fall of 1997, with approximately 10 million members, AOL was handling roughly 130 million Instant Messages a day. (And this was before Netscape had released its bundled version of the software.) That's an average of 13 Instant Messages a day for each AOL member. If we assume that only about 10 percent of AOL's membership uses the system on a given day, that's an average of 130 Instant Messages a day for each user! And the use will only grow: AOL now has 11 million members[3] and Netscape has approximately 68 million users of its Navigator Web browser.[4]

There is no real-world equivalent of this cyberspace capability. Instant Messaging allows us to know, automatically, in real time, when someone is accessible in cyberspace, regardless of where he or she is in real space. This aspect of Instant Messaging is qualitatively different from the use of the telephone. There are many benefits of this capability: It will give people new ways to shop together online, do homework together online, or do whatever else might require real-time communication. But it also adds an extraordinary layer of surveillance to the process of communication that is unlike any other in our society—which leads to the next common theme.

The Internet and Societal "Slack"

The impact of computers and the Internet on personal privacy is not a new subject. When I worked at ARPA/IPT, my other project (in addition to the ARPAnet) was related to privacy and security of computer and communications systems. Willis Ware of the Rand Corporation—one of the most well-known figures in the field in those early days—had a particularly insightful way of describing this issue: Ware talked of the ability of the computer systems that we were building to reduce the amount of "slack" that we expected in society.

As an example, how would you feel if an electronic message containing your license plate number and a description of your car were to be transmitted to the local police station every time the car that you were driving exceeded the speed limit? "Not reasonable," you might protest. "Too much 'Big Brother.'" Yet, a police officer driving behind you is already able to acquire the same information and relay it to the police station. "But that's different," you might argue. Why?

The concept of "privacy," as society has come to understand it, involves more than just limiting the dissemination of confidential information. Privacy also encompasses the notion that our activities, and information about our activities, ought to be protected, to be "kept private." We don't want all publicly available information automatically recorded, let alone made available to others. We like the slack in the system. And in some cases—such as driving above the speed limit—we like the ability to stretch the rules with a high probability that we won't get caught. The issue of computers and privacy is not a new issue, but the Internet, and other computer and communications technologies, are bringing about qualitative changes in the balances that we have come to expect.

The Internet and Users' Personas

While the previous points may have conjured fears of George Orwell's *1984*, such a view of the future is unlikely to prove accurate. At the same time that the Internet is tightening the slack on society, it is also creating (or at least loosening) slack in human behavior, because the Internet fosters free play of one's persona.

Much of adult life is spent doing the "proper" thing in the "proper" way. The Internet allows a return to the pliability of adolescence, a freedom to assume identities and behaviors that moves beyond the children's games and virtual reality publicized by the popular press. On the Internet, one can behave in alternative ways that might not be acceptable in the real world, but that can be completely acceptable in a well-defined area of cyberspace. Certainly, some behaviors are as unacceptable on the Internet as they are in "real" life, but this fact does not negate the very real and positive aspects of this kind of virtual freedom.

While anti-social behavior on the Internet dominates public discussion, it is only one possibility. To give just one more positive example, I recently received an e-mail notifying me that a business acquaintance had listed me as one of his connections on the "sixdegrees" Web site.[5] I knew nothing about this Web site, but my first reaction was to feel flattered, because I had been referred by someone I did not know well but would like to know better. Curious, I visited the site, which essentially interlinks or "networks" people. Although I had the option of not participating in this human networking, I ultimately chose to register (although I limited the amount of personal information that I was willing to have listed in the site's White Pages). In doing so, I had agreed to participate in an online form of networking that I would have probably found embarrassing had I been at a cocktail party. The presumed anonymity of the Internet actually enticed me to "try it out," especially because I could always remove my listing if I desired. (Incidentally, within twenty-four hours I had received e-mail on various subjects that were of interest to me from people who were "networked" by the site to me. But don't let me spoil your fun; go to the site and make your own decision of whether or not to try it.)

Who among us has not sent e-mail to someone we would hesitate to telephone? Who among us has not received e-mail—and I don't mean junk e-mail—from someone we know but would have preferred not to hear from? Behavior is different in cyberspace. And the usual first reaction to the parts of a new behavior that make us uncomfortable is to call for someone to fix them, to bring things back to the way they were—which leads to the next common theme.

The Internet and New Models

As the full dimensions of the Internet's impact and implications begin to emerge, much of the current discussion centers on the need for new models. The Internet raises issues that cannot be resolved by conventional approaches, whether by the private or public sectors. Consider, for example, some of the issues of everyday commerce: regulation of financial services, movement of money, product liability, advertising claims, choice of laws, settlements, contracts, and taxation. Regardless of whether we are philosophically inclined toward more or less government regulation, the ways we treat these issues in real space and in cyberspace are likely to become vastly different. While it is easy to describe some of the problems to be solved within any specific issue, and easy to note that one approach or another will not work, it is much more difficult to come up with the new models that will form the basis for solutions to those problems, models that may be fundamentally different from those we live by today.

If the Internet affects these commercial issues, for example, and if it undercuts the role of government as profoundly as some believe it will, who will build the roads? It is increasingly common to claim that the global medium of the Internet is enabling us to act locally. But how can it do that at the same time as it challenges some of the foundations of our local institutions, such as their ability to function effectively as taxing authorities? While several of the authors of this volume make admirable attempts to frame these and similar questions, finding answers to the questions will challenge society in the years ahead, which leads to the final common theme.

The Internet and Growth

In the past, the traditional view of organizations, especially in the private sector, tended to be that bigger was better. Companies tried to grow. Size mattered. But the Internet changes our notions of big vs. small, fast vs. slow. In the case of the Internet, it is speed that matters, not size. And speed, along with agility, tends to manifest itself in smaller, not larger, entities. The past decades have seen many new companies, often started by young people, effectively challenging the bigger, older, more staid organizations.

But evidence is mounting to complicate the issue, evidence that suggests that the successful speedy tend to become big. Economists now recognize the phenomenon of *increasing returns*, a concept that embodies the fact that the incremental cost of making and selling some products (copies of software, for example) is marginal. The more product that is sold, the greater the percentage of the revenues that are also profits. We know that a small company can thus become a Microsoft in the offline world, but does the same law apply to the Internet? Can an Amazon.com, for example, become so effective, so well known, at selling books on the Internet that it crowds out competition, and acquires a disproportionately larger share of the market than it might have acquired in the real world? Will there be fewer successful "book stores" on the Internet than there are in the real world? Will a successful online player be able to succeed in the real world as well? Is success in the real world even necessary for a cyberspace company?

* * *

Although each of the following chapters focuses on a particular topic area, each struggles with these and other common themes. In a sense, all six chapters address a few central questions: How dramatic an impact will the Internet have on the main institutions of our society? Will the Internet be a new tool for achieving existing goals, or will it produce fundamental changes in these institutions and thus force us to redefine our expectations of them? How will these institutions carry out the process of adjusting their relationships with newly empowered individuals and organizations?

The most profound quality of the Internet is its ability to democratize, that is, to put power in the hands of citizens, consumers, and members of various groups. While the Internet threatens the hierarchical nature of society as we know it today, and will no doubt have a profound impact on existing communities, it also enables new hierarchies and new communities. The Internet is reshaping our world—even if no one knows quite how.

THE CHAPTERS

The Institute for Information Studies commissioned the chapters for this book from various experts in the field; the designated authors prepared preliminary versions of their articles for distribution before the conference. At the conference itself, the authors presented brief synopses of their work, emphasizing the points they believed important. The invited reviewers and the other authors then critiqued each early draft. The discussions were creative and thought provoking; the authors were gracious and open minded. In each case, discussion tended in two directions: focused attention paid to material the author(s) included, and wide-ranging suggestions for the incorporation of material outside the authors' own focus. In the months following the conference, the authors revised their articles to produce the chapters of this book.

It is easy to be a critic; it is hard to be an artist. It is easy to comment upon someone else's essay; it is hard to write an essay oneself. And when it comes to aspects of the Internet, it is virtually impossible to cover in one essay, one chapter, or even one book, all of the various interrelated issues that make for a coherent analysis. But if each author had been given a book to fill—and a year to write—I expect that he or she might have explored even more issues related to the same themes discussed above.

Chapter 1: Sovereignty in the Networked World

This first chapter, by Michael R. Nelson, sets the tone for the volume by exploring how the "digital revolution" is affecting the ways in which nations connect to their citizens, their economies, and their national cultures.

As has been the case (to a lesser degree) with all previous media, the Internet makes national borders less and less relevant. Governments are losing control of many of the events and behaviors that are central to their power: taxation, national culture, telecommunications, movement of ideas, citizens' identities, capital, and national policy. This loss of control occurs with respect not only to citizens' actions, but also to the information they may get from the media and each other. Information technology has put power and choice in the hands of individuals who no longer need to rely on the government for information, solutions to problems, or decision making.

Optimists will find this new situation encouraging, if governments are willing to adjust to their reduced roles and resources. This chapter contains some constructive ideas for how governments can, in fact, adapt to the networked world. For instance, Nelson suggests that partnerships between citizens and businesses are a new model which will take years to build, but will allow for the continued transformation of the global economy and international political system.

Pessimists are likely to concentrate on the challenges for governments that will find it difficult to deal with these issues both internally and across borders. Answering these challenges will require a new generation of global leaders—ones who will have come of age in the information age—to resist the enormous pressure for greater nationalism and protectionism. Those new leaders must find new models for government as well as new approaches to governing.

Chapter 2: The New "Civic Virtue" of the Internet

David R. Johnson and David G. Post present a creative approach to solving the problem of creating laws and governance for the online world. They argue that the best approach to governing the Internet is to treat each separate online location as a distinct, self-governing *place*, with its own rules governing actions that primarily affect its own participants.

In their vision, would-be regulators of the Internet should keep their hands off and "let it emerge" into separate, virtual communities governed by rules that are negotiated by the participants. They call this type of governance a new form of "civic virtue" because the rulers do not impose the rules; instead, the rules arise from the ruled.

Some may question this notion that online communities with their own rules and regulations provide a superior model to our offline form of common government. This view—that there can be no single shared vision of the common good in cyberspace—is at odds with the history of government and institutions in the twentieth century. It is also at odds with current efforts to provide consistency and standards of decency across the whole Internet, from domain names to rules against hate speech. Many online advocates are currently worried that the Internet will never grow into a full consumer medium if it retains this kind of wild-west, frontier mentality (an outcome that would be fine with many of the Internet's earliest advocates, who have always preferred its relative anarchy).

But for those who are interested in the growing movement to limit the regulation of the Internet, this proposal to allow each of its unique, virtual communities to regulate itself offers a real challenge: How will these communities operate?

Chapter 3: The Internet and Community
In this chapter, Jeffrey Abramson calls into question two common metaphors for the Internet. The first is that its users are lone "surfers" who flit from site to site; on the contrary, Abramson shows, a majority of users habitually and repeatedly visit the same sites, digging in as if they were "homesteaders." At the same time, though, those homesteaders do not inhabit anything like the "global village" the Internet is said to represent; as discussed in the previous chapter, the Internet turns out to be not one homogeneous village, but rather hundreds of thousands of unique communities, each with its own unique interests and forms of communication. Because those virtual communities replicate both the possibilities and problems of geographically defined communities, a major challenge for existing institutions will be to deal with the tendency of online communities to become insular—a result of their citi-

zens' habits of frequenting only those communities or sites that interest them or support their views.

As the Internet breaks down geographic boundaries that have previously defined community, it is tempting to think that the result will be global experience requiring the creation of global institutions. Certainly, companies and countries have all focused their energies on going global. But the catch-phrase "think globally, act locally" may be a good model for the Internet, which seems to operate that way; interestingly, this essentially global medium seems to work best at its most molecular level: the community.

Chapter 4: Will the Internet Transform Higher Education?

This chapter, by Walter S. Baer, takes the issue of the Internet's impact on institutions and communities into the heart of a central example: higher education. Peter Drucker and others have predicted that in thirty years the university as we know it will no longer exist. For the short run, however, Baer concludes that the Internet will probably augment higher education more than it will transform it, because the Internet is still too new, too costly, and perhaps too threatening to bring about major change any time soon. He also argues that regulation, bureaucracy, tradition, and turf will block its more revolutionary potential.

The more likely scenario, Baer argues, is that the Internet will provide "better, faster, cheaper" additions to existing academic structures and traditions, as well as open the playing fields of higher education to private-sector firms, sometimes in cooperation and sometimes in competition with academic institutions. But whether or not one agrees with the argument that the Internet's benefits of cost savings and distance learning will have little fundamental effect on higher education, it is indisputable that the Internet is becoming a vehicle for training and education, particularly for non-degreed students.

Chapter 5: The Internet and Electronic Commerce: A Tale of Three Cities

While educators and entrepreneurs are only beginning to gauge the potential of the Internet for higher education, boosters of electronic commerce are already showing us its usefulness and challenging us to predict how far its impact will go. As author Elliot Maxwell notes, even a ten percent increase in electronic commerce would make a huge difference in the global economy. While many observers have focused on how the growth of electronic commerce will affect consumers, individual companies, or industries, Maxwell focuses instead on the effects of governments—particularly those with taxing authority—on electronic commerce.

The United States is not alone in developing policies regarding online commerce; governments around the world are struggling to develop policy frameworks to accommodate this new reality. In 1997, the United States, Japan, and the European Union released papers on the digital economy. All three recognize three truths: Internet development has positive benefits for society; the Internet is a global institution; and the Internet raises new issues that require global resolution. All three also endorse a limited role for government in electronic commerce, a key and somewhat surprising victory for wise decision making.

Still, tough questions remain about the desire of governments at all levels to tax electronic commerce. Local jurisdictions in particular are fearful of losing a valuable tax base if a portion of local commerce shifts to the Web. The tax moratorium that has been proposed in the United States, and proposals for Internet taxes in Europe are two very different solutions to the problem. This issue will be a test of each country's resolve to let markets, not governments, regulate the industry. Yet, as noted previously in this introduction, there are many issues that neither governments nor private entities can resolve alone, but which must nevertheless be resolved if electronic commerce is to function effectively. More significantly, most of these issues cannot be resolved in one country alone.

Chapter 6: Development and the Globalization of Cyberspace

As has been noted throughout each of the previous chapters, the global nature of the Internet poses challenges for institutions of all kinds. The final chapter of this volume, by Heather E. Hudson, raises concerns about the desire of many governments to limit access to information for the majority of their citizens. Perceiving danger and destabilization in the Internet's ability to link their citizens to individuals and organizations across the world, these governments attempt to restrict access through telecommunications policies and other laws intended to control information exchange. Because clever users will always be able to find the means to bypass such restrictions, this has the effect of creating classes of information "haves" and "have-nots"/ "knows" and "know-nots."

In the absence of such rearguard actions, the Internet can be a tool for positive outcomes. Hudson describes a number of international initiatives to make the Internet available in developing countries and to use these fledgling Internet programs to benefit the countries and their citizens. But the lessons of failure in these areas seem more illuminating than the successes. Too often, investments in technology alone have not resulted in major social change or benefits because the initiatives viewed technology as a goal, not a tool. When too little thought is given to the applications the technology is to support, it cannot succeed. Services are then often perceived as "frills" and pilot projects build no lasting constituency.

The globalization of cyberspace should not be judged by these tests, however. Used appropriately, cyberspace can break down borders and create new opportunities. It can be a means for countries and their citizens to learn from each other, to communicate, and to transcend differences. Narrow definitions of the role of cyberspace in development terms will block that objective.

THE EMERGING FUTURE

In just the past year, the Internet has undeniably become a mainstream phenomenon. Shopping on the Internet has become acceptable, and is increasing. The Internet has become a growing part of the educational experience (perhaps it's just a reflection of where we live, but my kids now routinely get homework assignments that specifically require them to obtain information on the Internet). And governments, as well as companies, now openly factor the Internet into their plans and policies. The Internet is here to stay. We have passed through the transition to a qualitative change in technology and in society. Or have we just entered the transition? Who knows?

If anything is clear, it is that our collective crystal balls are cloudy and our ability to foresee—let alone understand—the future is limited. The community affiliated with ARPA/IPT in the 1960s did not predict the Internet of today, and the experts and commentators of today are just as likely to fall short in their visions of where we will be in the next thirty years. And this points to the fundamental question raised in one way or another by all of the authors of this volume: Should we be seeking a vision of what the future *will be*, or should we be seeking a process for coping with the emerging future, however it unfolds?

Today, the Internet remains only a partially integrated phenomenon; cyberspace is still a place apart. In the future, however, the Internet will be part of a person's daily routine and an organization's daily operations, much as e-mail has already become routine for many of us. The first challenge—on which most observers, including the authors of this volume, tend to focus—is the challenge of developing a vision of what that new Internet-enabled society and life will be like. The greater challenge, it seems to me, is to understand the evolutionary path and the transitional strategies that will be necessary to guide us from where we are today to any Internet-related vision of tomorrow.

What makes this point in human history so interesting is that we are all—people, organizations, and governments—struggling with the vast changes in our processes and procedures that the Internet is bringing about, and will continue to bring about. The challenge is not to predict the end point of the change—namely, what the Internet-enabled future will be—but rather to better understand what we must do today and tomorrow, no matter what the Internet becomes or brings about.

We are notoriously poor at predicting the future, but perhaps we can develop better policies for the journey toward it. Perhaps the next Aspen Institute conference will ask not what the Internet *is*, or what the Internet's impact *will be*, but rather what people and institutions can do to cope with the changes the Internet will bring, however it emerges.

Arthur A. Bushkin
President & Chief Operating Officer
Pace Financial Network, L.L.C.
and
President
Galway Partners, L.L.C.
January 1998

ENDNOTES

1. John Hindle, "The Internet as Paradigm: Phenomenon and Paradox," introduction to *The Internet as Paradigm* (Washington, D.C.: The Aspen Institute, 1997), vii.
2. AOL's Instant Messenger now appears as an embedded feature in Netscape's Navigator Web browser. And this technology will spread; already IBM's Lotus (Notes) and Qualcomm (Eudora) are additional licensees.
3. This figure is of January 1998, prior to the completion of AOL's acquisition of CompuServe.
4. As reported in the *San Francisco Chronicle*, 20 January 1998.
5. See http://www.sixdegrees.com.

SOVEREIGNTY IN THE NETWORKED WORLD

Michael R. Nelson

**Director, Technology Policy, Office of Plans and Policy
Federal Communications Commission**

Valentine's Day 1996 marked the fiftieth anniversary of ENIAC, the first digital, electronic computer.[1] The invention of ENIAC launched the computer revolution, which has provided the inexpensive computing power on which hundreds of millions of people rely every day in offices and classrooms, and at supermarket checkout counters and automatic teller machines. Steady, rapid decreases in the cost of computing have already transformed business around the globe and are now transforming education, entertainment, and government. But the computer revolution is just the prelude to what has been called the *digital revolution,*[2] the result of advances in digital telecommunications technologies that—by linking together millions of computers and other "information appliances"—are multiplying the power of computers and dramatically increasing humanity's ability to effectively and affordably utilize information.

This digital revolution is having profound consequences. In *The Third Wave,* Alvin Toffler describes three fundamental transformations in the economic and social structure of civilization.[3] The "First Wave" resulted from the invention of agriculture; the second was brought on by the industrial revolution. The "Third Wave" is a social and economic restructuring made possible by information technology, biotechnology,

The opinions and conclusions of this paper are those of the author and do not necessarily reflect the views of the Federal Communications Commission (FCC), any of its Commissioners, or other members of the FCC staff.

and new energy technologies. But while the impact of the agricultural revolution spread over more than a thousand years, and the industrial revolution lasted more than a hundred years, the digital revolution—which is likely to be even more far-reaching in effect—is taking place in just decades. As U.S. President Bill Clinton has noted, this digital revolution is "changing the way we work, the way we live, the way we relate to each other. Already the revolution is so profound it is changing the dominant economic model of the age."[4] Indeed, the digital revolution is leading to a fundamental restructuring of world economies, governments, and entire societies.

The impact of the Internet, which is accelerating the digital revolution, can be compared to that of the printing press in the 1400s and 1500s. The development of the printing press gave nearly every citizen in Europe access to the printed page and encouraged widespread literacy. In time, it also encouraged political activism. The Declaration of Independence, which played a critical role in uniting the thirteen American colonies in a common purpose, had its crystallizing impact only because dozens of newspapers throughout the colonies printed and distributed thousands of copies of it. Indeed, many historians have concluded that the free flow of information unleashed by the printing press made possible the Protestant Reformation and the Thirty Years' War, the growth of capitalism and the nation state, and the Glorious Restoration in England in 1688, the American Revolution in 1776, and the French Revolution in 1789.[5] Certainly, it is hard to imagine any of these developments in the absence of the relatively quick dissemination of information (e.g., religious tracts, propaganda, newspaper reports, and manifestos) made possible by the printing press.

We can hope that the sweeping changes spurred by the new digital technologies will not be as wrenching and as violent as those fueled by the printing press. While it is not possible to foresee all of the consequences of the digital revolution, forecasters can seek to understand the major technological trends, how these new digital technologies may be used, and how existing institutions will have to adapt.

This essay examines the ways in which the digital revolution will affect national governments, challenge definitions of "sovereignty," and lead to fundamental changes in the roles and powers of governments. Rather than attempt to predict the future of technology, this chapter presents a scenario of how a *networked world* may evolve, and then examines the consequences for government. In particular, this essay explores how power and control will shift away from governments toward the private sector and to individual citizens. The essay concludes with some thoughts on how the U.S. government and other governments can best adapt to the new realities of a networked world.

A SCENARIO FOR THE NETWORKED WORLD

The Global Business Network and its founder, Peter Schwartz, have been very successful in constructing scenarios for companies and governments around the world and exploring the implications of these possible worlds. Schwartz's book, *The Art of the Long View*, is an invaluable guide to business forecasting in the face of dramatic, unpredictable technological change.[6] In recent years, Schwartz and other members of the Global Business Network have published important work using scenarios to assess the impact of information technology on business and society.[7] I draw from this work as well as from a number of other recent books—e.g., Michael Dertouzos' *What Will Be* and Frances Cairncross' *The Death of Distance*—whose authors have documented the development and spread of digital technologies and speculated on how information technology and the telecommunications market will evolve.[8] Equally useful have been works of speculative fiction such as *Neuromancer* by William Gibson, *Snow Crash* by Neal Stephenson, and *Earth* by David Brin, which explore the ways in which these powerful technologies will affect the people who use them.[9]

How the future will unfold is anybody's guess; while a short-term extrapolation of current technological trends is relatively straightforward, a prediction of how quickly new technologies will diffuse into everyday use is more difficult. And it is impossible to foresee the startling new ways in which the new technologies will be used; ten years ago—even five years ago—for example, no one could have predicted the explosive growth of the World Wide Web. The author of this paper can therefore make only educated guesses about the further evolution of the information-technology and telecommunications marketplace.

Still, mindful of the inherent limitations and dangers in such an undertaking, we can construct a plausible scenario to illustrate some of the ways in which information and telecommunications technologies will be used ten years from now. This scenario builds upon a classic Silicon Valley maxim, "That which is possible is inevitable." Where a technology or application exists today, I have assumed that in the long term—i.e., ten years (which equals at least thirty Internet years, according to the Silicon Valley calendar)—there will be no effective barriers to its widespread utilization.

This scenario also assumes the continued strength of two drivers of the digital revolution. The first is competition. To date, the development and deployment of computer technology have been spurred by vigorous, unrestricted competition in the computer hardware and software industries and in many of the industries that are the heaviest users of computer technology (e.g., manufacturing, financial markets). This scenario assumes that the accelerating trend towards liberalization and deregulation of the telecommunications sector both in the United States and abroad will continue and lead to a similar rapid deployment of new digital telecommunications technologies.

The second driver of the computer revolution has been the extraordinary and steady advances in chip technology quantified in "Moore's Law," Gordon Moore's empirical observation that the number of transistors that manufacturers can place on a chip doubles about every eighteen months.[10] A corollary of Moore's Law—that the cost of transistors on a computer chip decreases by fifty percent every eighteen months—has been remarkably accurate for more than thirty years. Similar dramatic reductions in the cost of data storage are also occurring. And with the advent of real competition throughout the telecommunications sector, it is quite likely that the cost of digital communications will also begin to follow a similar trajectory. After all, today's digital networks are composed of digital switches that rely on the same type of computer chips and software used in computers. Furthermore, the communications industry relies on the same type of technical talent as the computer industry. Thus, by extrapolating from current technological trends, it is possible to predict with some confidence that, over the next decade, the costs of digital communications, data storage, and information services will decrease at least as rapidly as the cost of computing power.

If we assume that the digital revolution continues and even accelerates, by the year 2008 we can expect developments in the following seven areas:

- *Cheap computing power.* Computing power will be at least 100 times less expensive than today. That means that computers with the capabilities of today's top-of-the-line multimedia workstations (high-quality digital sound, videoconferencing, and the ability to store, search, and display gigabytes of information) will be available for the equivalent of a couple of hundred dollars. Whether such a device is called a PC, a network computer, or a smart toaster, it will be much easier to use than today's systems and may even include voice-recognition capabilities that would obviate the need for a keyboard.

- *Choice of service providers.* In most developed countries, many developing countries, and almost every major metropolitan center, business customers will have a range of telecommunications service providers from which to chose. While there may still be limited choice for wireline service, a variety of wireless and satellite services will provide affordable local and international connections. In the case of callback services and many satellite services, the service provider will be able to completely bypass the local telecommunications carrier and will be beyond the control of any national government.

- *Cheap communications.* Communications costs will decrease dramatically in those countries and for those services where real competition exists. Arthur C. Clarke's novel *2061* describes how on 31 December 2000, "every telephone call became a local one, and the human race greeted the new millennium by transforming itself into one huge, gossiping family."[11] Thanks to Internet telephony, this transformation may cease being science fiction relatively soon—if not by the end of the year 2000, then at least by 2008. If the telecommunications industry learns to take full advantage of Moore's Law, the cost of moving a bit of information a kilometer will shrink by 95 to 99 percent. Nor will it be inconceivable—one day soon—for companies to offer free worldwide phone calls to customers who buy bandwidth-intensive services such as videoconferencing, just as some cable companies in the United Kingdom now offer free local phone service to new subscribers. By 2008, videoconferencing should be as inexpensive as it is to send a fax today. High-speed data networks will have spread to at least as many people as use telephone today and low-earth-orbiting satellite systems such as Iridium and Teledesic will ensure universal—if costly—service to every corner of the globe.

- *Cyber-commerce.* Electronic commerce over the Internet will account for a significant portion of the global economy, at least 5 percent and perhaps more than 10 percent. According to recent estimates, about $10 billion of transactions took place over the Internet in 1997. This represents approximately half of 1 percent of the global economy,[12] but forecasts predict growth over the next few years ranging from spectacular to unprecedented. A recent article from the *Economist* estimated that business-to-business electronic commerce could exceed $100 billion by the year 2000.[13] According to projections from International Data Corporation, the global online market could equal $220 billion by 2001.[14] Every reason exists to expect such explosive growth to continue for many years. By 2008, software, video, professional services, data services, government services, and newspapers and magazines will all be routinely delivered electronically, not only in the United States, but throughout Europe, in Japan, and many countries of the developing world as well.

- *Online labor.* Worldwide, hundreds of millions of "knowledge workers" will spend much or all of their work days online, engaged in videoconferencing sessions, collaborating on documents with colleagues around the world, and accessing huge digital libraries of information. A significant portion of them will be able to work from home or wherever they please rather than commuting to the office every day. Already today, more than 11 million Americans telecommute. That number has tripled since 1990 and is growing rapidly, spurring deployment of high-speed telecommunications technology such as ISDN, xDSL, and cable modems.[15]

- *Security.* Driven by the growth of electronic commerce and the need for security and reliability, strong effective means of encryption and digital signatures will become widespread. These technologies will enable users to transfer money electronically, sign electronic contracts, and confidentially share information.

- *Anonymity.* Users of the Internet will be able to transact business online either anonymously or using a pseudonym. Today, several sites on the Internet allow users to send untraceable electronic mail.[16] In the future, anonymous digital cash will be commonplace and transportable across national borders via the Internet, allowing anonymous payments for goods and services.

While this scenario is incomplete and may overlook some of the most exciting applications of information technology, and while no one can know whether the developments predicted will occur in five, ten, or fifteen years, a scenario such as this can be a very useful tool in assessing how government institutions will need to change if they are going to survive (and even contribute to) the digital revolution.

IMPLICATIONS FOR NATIONAL SOVEREIGNTY

Webster's defines "sovereignty" simply as "supreme power especially over a body politic; dominion; freedom from external control; autonomy." In 1949, in one of the first cases of the Permanent Court of International Justice—the Corfu Channel Case—the judge defined sovereignty as "the whole body of rights and attributes which a State possesses in its territory, to the exclusion of all other States, and also in its relations with other States. Sovereignty confers rights upon States and imposes obligations on them."[17]

Throughout history, governments and citizens alike have sought to preserve their countries' sovereignty and power. Few countries today wield the kind of "supreme power" that a king or queen or even a parliament might have enjoyed a hundred years ago. A networked world further complicates the concept of sovereignty. Networks breed interdependence; the digital revolution is making national borders less and less relevant as it requires national governments to cooperate with other governments when formulating both foreign and domestic policies.[18] The growth of global information networks, the power of the transnational corporations that run them, and the creation of a truly global electronic market will mean that national governments will no longer be able to exercise many of their prerogatives under the concept of sovereignty, such as controlling citizens' telecommunications options, the content of public and private communications, national culture, movement of expertise and ideas, citizens' identities, capital, taxation, and national policy.[19]

Control of Networks

As national telecommunications markets all over the world are opened to foreign investment, and foreign companies begin to build and control telecommunications networks, national governments will have less and less control over the telecommunications links that their citizens use. In Sweden, which was one of the first countries to fully open its telephone market to foreign competition, most of the national government's telecommunications needs are met by foreign companies. USWest is among the companies connecting Swedish government offices to each other and the rest of the world. A Singapore company provides phone service to the Swedish foreign ministry.

Global telecommunications satellite systems, such as those being built by Iridium and ICO, will enable citizens of a country to make phone calls and connect to the Internet using a telecommunications network completely outside the borders of their country and beyond the control of their national government. This situation has its benefits and drawbacks. If governments cannot listen in on the conversations of its citizens, dissidents will be better able to publicize their causes and oppose oppressive regimes. If, however, governments cannot use wiretaps, they will have a much harder time detecting and tracking transnational terrorist and criminal groups.

To maintain their ability to wiretap telephone lines for criminal investigations or intelligence collection, national governments will need either new technological approaches or the cooperation of the foreign company that controls the telecommunications links. Before the U.S. government would consider approving the proposed British Telecom–MCI merger, for example, the new company had to enter into an agreement with the U.S. Federal Bureau of Investigation to ensure that American law enforcement agencies would retain their ability to wiretap the networks of the new, foreign-owned company.[20]

Control of Content

Even in those cases in which national governments arrange with national foreign carriers to retain some control over the telecommunications links used by their citizens, it is quite likely that encryption technologies will make it very hard for governments to decipher much of the telecommunications traffic they intercept. In effect, governments' successes in retaining control of the networks used by their citizens will become irrelevant once strong, effective encryption becomes widespread.

This loss of control means that governments will have less and less ability to influence and control the information their citizens get from the media and from each other. The use of faxes to link the dissidents in Tiananmen Square with supporters around the world, the use of the Internet by Zapitista guerrillas in Mexico to promote their cause and by the Serbian radio station B92 in Belgrade to avoid censorship and radio jamming are early indications of how new technologies are making it increasingly difficult for governments to control the flow of information.

The fact that new digital video technologies, when coupled with the Internet, allow anyone with a few thousand dollars to broadcast not only text, but still images and even video clips to a worldwide audience of millions of the most influential and "well-connected" people around the planet cannot be underestimated. Ten years ago, it would have cost millions of dollars to reach such an audience. Consider the impact of a short, grainy videotape showing the beating of Rodney King, which led to a months-long nationwide debate in the United States over police brutality. Now consider the potential impact of millions of people around the globe armed with digital video cameras and Internet connections.

National Culture

Any technology that breaks down cultural barriers will be seen by many as a threat to their national cultures and identities. The worldwide popularity of Hollywood movies and videos and American music is often considered to be a threat to indigenous cultures, especially in small countries and countries in which less common languages are spoken. The digital revolution promises to deliver an almost unlimited variety of video programming and music to anyone who connects to the Internet. In the worst of all possible worlds, a few mega-conglomerates could determine what the whole world watches. But because the Internet reduces the costs of producing and distributing programming to almost zero, it is likely to make decentralization—not concentration—the rule. As a result, more—and more varied—programming will be available to all. Today in Los Angeles, Iranian emigres can watch Iranian television programs on the local cable television network. In the future, programming in hundreds of different languages from thousands of different cultures and traditions will be available and affordable online.

Whether globalization will pose a threat to native cultures is unclear. I believe it is far more likely to strengthen and promote cultural identity by enabling a larger, more dispersed community to experience the richness of a particular culture. But others fear that least-common-denominator programming (probably in English) will come to dominate cyberspace, just as it dominates the cinema and television broadcasting in many countries. Such fears could lead national governments to attempt to restrict or tax foreign content imported into their countries. Of course, given the decentralized nature of the Internet, such efforts may prove difficult or futile.

Movement of Expertise and Ideas

Governments have often tried to discourage or prevent the migration of their best and brightest citizens. "Brain drain" continues to be a serious concern in many developing countries. The Internet will render meaningless efforts by governments to control the movement of their citizens. When it is easy and affordable for almost anyone to use the Internet or the telephone network for a high-quality, international videoconference, millions of workers will live in one country and work in another. Go into cyberspace and you can work anywhere you wish. While governments may continue to use visas and passports to track and limit the international travel of their citizens, it won't matter. Software developers, consultants, and doctors, as well as money launderers, pornographers, and drug dealers, will all go on the Internet to conduct business with colleagues and customers around the world.

Anonymity

Today, anonymous remailers allow Internet users to send a message to a third party who will strip off all indications of the sender's identity before sending it onto the intended recipient. In some cases, such remailers have been used by pedophiles and others to distribute illegal materials and stolen information and engage in other illegal or questionable activities. In the future, at least a few online bankers and merchants will also allow a wide range of anonymous financial transactions. By allowing such anonymous transactions, the Internet will make it much harder for governments to monitor the activities— whether legal or illegal—of their citizens.

Control of Capital

Combining anonymity with the instantaneous ability to move millions of dollars of electronic cash across national borders will make it much more difficult for national governments to restrict or even monitor the movement of capital. This in turn will challenge the ability of central banks to control the value of national currencies. Already, today, several thousand currency traders can move billions of dollars a day, undermining the efforts of central banks to stabilize the value of currencies. How much more difficult will it be for central banks to track currency flows and influence the value of their national currencies when millions of Internet users can move money as easily as the largest international banks do today?

Taxation

The fact that electronic money will make borders even more porous to the movement of money, thus undermining the ability of national governments to track money flow, will have serious implications for tax collection. A recent article in the *Economist* on the "disappearing taxpayer" describes how wealthy individuals are realizing that a networked world allows them to easily move their assets to countries with the most favorable tax rates.[21] This trend means that governments will have an increasingly difficult time collecting many of the tax monies upon which they rely. It will not be easy to collect tariffs on goods imported over the Internet. Nor will it be clear how a national government would calculate the tax owed by a citizen who runs a virtual business that sells software or services online to customers around the world using a sales force (or even electronic agents) and servers in dozens of countries. How will governments stop their most successful online entrepreneurs from incorporating their businesses and setting up their servers in a tax haven in the Caribbean or elsewhere? A U.S. Department of Treasury paper published in November 1996 explores many of these issues but poses far more questions than it answers.[22] This paper is being used as the basis for discussions among finance officials of the G10 nations on tax issues posed by electronic commerce.[23]

Control of National Policy

As the Internet makes capital and expertise increasingly mobile, governments will come under a corresponding pressure to adopt tax policies and other policies that are similar, if not identical, to those of their major trading partners. The development of a networked world is a driving force behind many of the recent agreements at the World Trade Organization (WTO), as well as the increasing integration of the European Union and the growth of free-trade zones in North and South America. When online companies can relocate million-dollar operations in a few days, governments have to be more responsive than ever to the complaints of corporate leaders and international nongovernmental organizations (NGOs). As Jessica Mathews wrote recently in *Foreign Affairs*, NGOs as varied as Greenpeace, the Red Cross, and the International Chamber of Commerce will have a growing influence over governmental policies.[24] And as Walter Wriston, former chairman of Citibank, has noted: "Money goes where it is wanted and stays where it is well-treated."[25]

On an increasing number of policy issues, whether telecommunications regulation or trade policy, governments are being driven to harmonize policies by international business groups and other nongovernmental organizations. In many cases, these international groups persuade corporations or organizations in dozens of countries to agree on a common set of recommendations; these corporations and organizations then persuade their home governments to adopt the recommendations. Particularly on technical and standards-related issues, such private-sector–led efforts are quite common. This process has been accelerated by the evolution of multinational companies into transnational companies that can often exert simultaneous political pressure in all the countries in which they operate. In the 1960s, multinational companies were rather tightly linked to their home countries. Today, more and more transnational companies are becoming almost "anational"— able to operate successfully regardless of what actions their home countries might take. In such corporations, many employees may feel more loyalty to the firm than to their own countries.

IMPLICATIONS OF THIS SCENARIO

So what will remain of the traditional idea of sovereignty if governments cannot require the allegiance of their citizens and are forced to tailor their domestic policies to meet the needs not only of their own citizens but of citizens and corporations throughout the world? Governments will no longer control the telecommunications networks and satellite telecommunications links their citizens use. Even where governments make arrangements to retain access to the content of their citizens' communication, the spread of encryption technology will make it increasingly difficult to decipher those communications. The growth of electronic commerce will make it increasingly difficult for governments to control the flow of money, influence the value of their currency, and track or prevent money-laundering and other criminal activities. The Internet will provide a means for anonymous transactions and enable "virtual aliens" to work wherever they please—and avoid taxes in the process.

So what is left for governments to control? Not much. They will continue to control the territory and national resources within their borders, but those resources will be less and less relevant to the well-being of citizens living in a digital world. Compare Hong Kong, an island-state with 5.8 million people, a total area of 1,075 square kilometers, no natural resources, and a Gross Domestic Product (GDP) of $126 billion (of which 81 percent is generated by services), with Iran, which covers 1.6 million square kilometers, has abundant oil reserves, a population of 66 million people, and a GDP of only $59 billion. In today's world, land mass and natural resources are far less important to economic development than are an efficient, limited, and stable government; an advanced information infrastructure; technical talent; and an effective legal system that fosters investment.

While government officials will express dismay over the loss of sovereignty caused by the digital revolution, in most cases governments are losing control over things they don't or shouldn't need to control. In the United States, for example, because of the First Amendment to the Constitution, government has not sought to control or limit what citizens hear from the media or from each other, except in limited cases (e.g., libel, pornography, slander, copyright theft). The United States is proof that nations can survive and thrive without the kind of press and speech restrictions that many governments have traditionally imposed. In other countries without the American tradition of freedom of speech, political leaders are coming to realize that the free flow of information is essential if their nation's companies are to succeed in the networked economy. Similarly, policymakers worldwide are realizing that for the global market to work most efficiently, capital and expertise must easily flow across borders.

In *Power Shift,* Alvin Toffler distinguishes between the need of governments to have the power to ensure "socially necessary order" for the benefit of their citizens, and the tendency of governments to seek to impose "surplus order"—"that excess order imposed not for the benefit of the society, but exclusively for the benefit of those who control the state."[26] It is clear that many of the powers that government will lose as a result of the digital revolution—the ability to control telecommunications networks, the media, the communications of their citizens, the movement of money, and the "national culture"—are not needed to ensure "socially necessary order." What is not clear is whether losing the ability to detect and monitor illegal communications and financial transactions will cause national governments to lose the ability to protect their citizens. Nor is it clear whether being forced to follow tax, trade, and environmental policies supported by foreign countries and transnational companies will cause national governments to find themselves unable to meet their citizens' expectations of protection from terrorism, drugs, unsafe products, and environmental pollution. The power of governments could erode very rapidly if money becomes so mobile and so impossible to track that implementing a fair, effective tax system becomes problematic.

So what remains of sovereignty? Hundreds of years ago, "sovereignty" was defined as the power of the king or queen over a realm and its subjects. Today, in an increasingly interdependent, interconnected, cross-owned economy, the concept is much more difficult to define. The best definition is probably that sovereignty is what citizens expect their national governments to control. In some countries, e.g., Singapore, that control may include the media (and pornography and seditious material on the Internet) and whether people may chew gum in public. In other countries, expectations of government are more limited. U.S. citizens, for example, expect government to provide a suitable environment for business, to protect us from crime and foreign attack, to take steps to help us educate and prepare children for adulthood, and to help those "who cannot help themselves"—the ill, the elderly, and the poor. It will be interesting to see how the U.S. government, and any government, can meet those expectations in a networked world where law enforcement, national defense, and taxation—core functions of government—may be increasingly difficult to accomplish.

Who will step in if national governments cannot meet the expectations of their citizens? Increasingly, the United States is witnessing a power shift both to local governments and to intergovernmental organizations such as the World Trade Organization. This phenomenon, which has been called "glocalization," is being enabled by information technology and driven by a number of different developments.

The "Reagan Revolution," the Republican takeover of Congress, and the Clinton administration's efforts to "reinvent government" have spurred efforts to devolve U.S. federal governmental responsibilities to state and local governments wherever possible. As a result, since 1993, the number of state government employees has increased by more than 647,000[27] while the number of federal government workers has dropped by 309,000.[28] Information technology has made this process easier by enabling local and state governments to get the information and expertise they need and to share resources and experiences among themselves. Less and less do state and local governments have to rely on the federal government for expertise, information, and coordination.

At the same time, national governments are having to turn to intergovernmental organizations to address global issues, such as trade, environmental problems (e.g., global climate change or ozone depletion), and allocation of global resources such as the radio spectrum. The growing interdependence of countries and companies is driving this trend and again, information technology is making it easier. Intergovernmental organizations such as the WTO, the Intergovernmental Panel of Climate Change, or the International Telecommunications Union all depend critically on fax machines, the Internet, and the World Wide Web. Many intergovernmental organizations are using these technologies to be more effective, more productive, and more agile. By more closely linking the representatives of national governments, these organizations have been able to more quickly achieve consensus and resolve disputes between governments. Indeed, many of the officials who represent their national governments at intergovernmental organizations find that they communicate more and agree more with their counterparts from other countries than they do with officials from other agencies within their own government.

This phenomenon has been particularly striking in the recent international debates on encryption. At a July 1997 meeting on electronic commerce in Bonn, European economics and industry ministers developed general agreement that export controls on encryption need to be relaxed in order to foster electronic commerce.[29] Yet at another high-level meeting a few weeks later, justice and interior ministry officials from the "P8" nations (the G7 plus Russia) meeting in Lyon discussed high-tech crime and agreed on the need to control the spread of strong encryption that would hinder wiretaps, police investigations, and intelligence collection.[30]

Even more important than "glocalization" is the shift—at all levels—of power from national governments to the private sector. National policies are increasingly being driven by corporations and NGOs from Greenpeace to the International Red Cross to the Catholic Church. Often, the private sector has been very effective at using new information technologies to build support and exert political pressure both nationally and internationally. The recently completed WTO negotiations on information technology and telecommunications were between governments, but they could never have been concluded if national and multinational companies had not worked together to pressure their governments to open their markets, an act which will lead to lower prices for computer equipment and telecommunications services. Organizations such as the International Chamber of Commerce and the World Economic Forum are taking an increasing role in building consensus among major corporations, who will then pressure national governments to follow their lead. Several intergovernmental organizations, including the International Telecommunication Union, the Organization for Economic Cooperation and Development, and others, are expanding the roles of representatives of private corporations and NGOs in their meetings and policy-making processes.

Still more important than the shift of power from governments to corporations and NGOs has been the increase in power of the individual citizen attributable to information and telecommunications technologies. Information technology has made possible greater information about and scrutiny of government and corporate actions; easy access to a global audience via the Internet, CNN, and other global media; more effective coordination and mobilization of individuals who care about a specific issue; and new ways for individuals to solve problems themselves rather than having to rely on governments to solve their problems for them.

One of the most memorable images of Tiananmen Square was that of a single man standing alone blocking the way of a Chinese Army tank. It seems likely that he would have been run over quickly had no news cameras been there to capture his action and broadcast it to the world.[31] Another less dramatic example of the power of individuals to affect public issues was the controversy over Shell Oil's plans to dispose of the Brent Spar oil platform in the North Sea. Greenpeace used the Internet to coordinate its offices and its members around the world to mobilize public opinion against Shell's plans.[32]

But perhaps the most important way in which information technology is shifting power from national governments and corporations to individuals is by giving users of computers and the Internet new tools for making their own decisions and solving their own problems. In the past, for example, parents who were concerned about the type of programming their children were seeing on television often demanded that government step in and restrict the amount of sex and violence that broadcasters could show. The U.S. Communications Decency Act (CDA) was an attempt to do the same thing for the Internet.[33] But the CDA was found unconstitutional because the Supreme Court concluded that censorship of the Internet is not the best way to protect children from adult content in cyberspace. Rather than rely on governments to use their power to censor the Internet, parents now can use filtering and rating systems to keep inappropriate content out of their own homes without infringing on the rights of others to see such material. As these systems become more effective and easier to use, they will reduce the pressure on governments to regulate the kinds of content available on the Internet.[34]

Electronic commerce will likewise reduce the role for government. Governments at both the state and national levels spend billions of dollars regulating various industries. Especially where monopolies dominate the market, as in the local telephone market, government regulators have traditionally sought to control prices and protect consumers. But electronic commerce will open markets, increase competition, and provide consumers with more information on the products and services they buy. If consumers have more choices and better information about which companies sell defective or substandard products, they will have less reason to turn to government to regulate the marketplace.

A recent survey on electronic commerce published in the *Economist* shows clearly that information technology will result in more informed customers with more choices and lower prices.[35] When consumers can easily shop with companies around the world, the balance of power will shift from the seller to the buyer. At the same time, local and national consumer-protection laws will no longer be very effective in protecting the buyer, so consumers will have to find ways to protect themselves. Online buyers' guides, like those provided by the Better Business Bureau or computer magazines,[36] are one valuable tool.

CONCLUSIONS

It is clear that faster and more powerful computers networked together by low-cost, high-capacity digital communications links are transforming the global economy. It is also clear that this development is challenging traditional concepts of national sovereignty and eroding the traditional power of nations.

To date, few countries and few U.S. government agencies seem to understand the full implications of the digital revolution and even fewer are preparing to undergo the transformation needed to address the challenges and seize the opportunities that the revolution could provide. Most governments are woefully unprepared to deal with the changes that global networks will bring to international relations and the global economy. If the U.S. government can come to understand how the digital revolution is changing the role of governments, it can help facilitate the inevitable transformation of the global economy and the international political system.

The *Framework for Global Electronic Commerce,* released by White House on 1 July 1997, indicates that the U.S. government, at the highest levels, understands that the explosive growth of the Internet is due to the fact that the U.S. government has not tried to control or regulate it.[37] Furthermore, the report states that governments should have a limited role in the evolution of the global electronic marketplace and urges the private sector to establish mechanisms for self-governance.[38] Similar reports are needed to redefine the (smaller) role of governments in foreign policy, law enforcement, and economic policy in the networked world.

Failure to grasp the impact of information and telecommunications technologies and failure to effectively utilize these technologies will make it difficult and perhaps impossible for the United States to realize its foreign-policy, economic, and national-security objectives in the coming years. Change is always disruptive and the change caused by the digital revolution is pervasive and fundamental. It also has the potential to be economically devastating and violent to those who try to resist the changes that information technologies are bringing rather than enjoy the digital revolution's many benefits. U.S. leadership is needed if this is to be avoided.

As a technological optimist, I agree with Walter Wriston, who says:

> Information technology has demolished time and distance, but instead of validating [George] Orwell's vision of Big Brother watching the citizen, just the reverse has happened; the citizen is watching Big Brother and so the virus of freedom, for which there is no antidote, is spread by myriad electronic networks to the four corners of the world. This information technology is changing the way we think about sovereignty, the way we work, and indeed the nature of the work we do.[39]

Like Wriston, I believe that the dramatic changes brought by the new information and telecommunications technologies will provide opportunities for fostering creativity, economic growth, and community, and that individual citizens, empowered by these technologies, will work together to seize these opportunities. In the end, governments can only delay, not prevent, these changes. Nothing improves unless it changes—and dramatic improvement requires dramatic change.

ENDNOTES

The ideas outlined in this paper were developed and revised as the result of discussions at the following conferences: Forum on the Role of Science and Technology in Promoting National Security and Global Security,[40] organized by the White House Office of Science and Technology Policy, Washington, D.C., 29–30 March 1995; annual meeting of the World Economic Forum, Davos, Switzerland, January 1996;

McCormick Foundation Conference on the Information Revolution and National Security,[41] July 1996; second annual meeting of the Aspen Institute Roundtable on International Telecommunications,[42] Berlin, Germany, 19–22 July 1996; Highland Forum meeting, Santa Fe Institute, August 1996; and the Harvard University Conference on "Visions and Frictions," 17–18 April 1997.

1. To commemorate the occasion of ENIAC's invention, the University of Pennsylvania and the Association of Computing Machinery held a conference on 14 February 1997, in Philadelphia. Details on the conference and ENIAC's history are available at http://www.seas.upenn.edu/~museum.

2. For instance, U.S. Vice President Al Gore referred to the "digital revolution" in his remarks on the campus of UCLA in Los Angeles on 11 January 1994. His speech is available online at http://www.whitehouse.gov/WH/EOP/OVP/other/superhig.txt.

3. Alvin Toffler, *The Third Wave* (New York: Bantam Books, 1981).

4. From remarks by President Clinton at the signing ceremony for the Telecommunications Act Conference Report, 8 February 1996, available online at http:\\library.whitehouse.gov.

5. See, for example, Elizabeth Eisenstein, *The Printing Press as an Agent of Change* (New York: Cambridge University Press, 1980).

6. Peter Schwartz, *The Art of the Long View—Planning for the Future in an Uncertain World* (New York: Doubleday, 1991).

7. E.g., Peter Schwartz and Peter Leyden, "The Long Boom—A History of the Future, 1980–2020," *Wired,* July 1997, 115+, available online at http://www.wired.com/wired/5.07/longboom.html; and Peter Schwartz, *The Logics of Change,* 1995 GBN Scenarios Book (Emeryville, Calif.: Global Business Network, 1995).

8. Michael Dertouzos, *What Will Be—How the New World of Information Technologies Will Change Our Lives* (San Francisco: HarperEdge, 1997); Frances Cairncross, *The Death of Distance* (Boston: Harvard Business School Publishing, 1997). See also Frances Cairncross, "A Connected World—A Survey of Telecommunications," *The Economist,* 13 September 1997, 56+, also available online at http://www.economist.com/editorial/freeforall/21-9-97/index.survey.html. A few other useful sources include Don Tapscott and Art Caston, *Paradigm Shift—The New Promise of Information Technology* (New York: McGraw-Hill, 1992); Don Tapscott, *The Digital Economy: Promise and Peril in the Age of Networked Intelligence* (New York: McGraw-Hill, 1995); and Esther Dyson, *Release 2.0—A Design for Living in the Digital Age* (New York: Broadway Books, 1997).

9. William Gibson, *Neuromancer* (New York: Ace, 1986); Neal Stephenson, *Snow Crash* (New York: Bantam, 1993); David Brin, *Earth* (New York: Bantam, 1991).

10. In 1965, Gordon Moore, then head of research at Fairchild Semiconductor, observed that the young chip industry's rapidly improving technology was enabling it to double, *each year,* the number of transistors manufacturers could place on a chip. In 1975, as industry advances slowed, Moore reviewed the data and found that chip density was doubling every two years. More than three decades of accumulating data have solidified—while adjusting—what is now known as "Moore's Law": Chip count consistently doubles about every eighteen

months. See Otis Port, Interview with Gordon Moore ("Gordon Moore's Crystal Ball"), *Business Week,* 23 June 1997, 66.

11. Arthur C. Clarke, *2061, Odyssey Three* (New York: Ballantine Books, 1987), 17.

12. Estimates are taken from "Internet Leapfrog: The Impact of the Internet on Global Economic Competition," a 1997 report of the International Data Corporation, available online at http://www.idc.com.

13. Christopher Anderson, "In Search of the Perfect Market—A Survey of Electronic Commerce," *The Economist,* 10 May 1997, p. 56+, available online at http://www.economist.com/editorial/freeforall/14-9-97/index.survey.html.

14. "Internet Leapfrog."

15. From a survey funded by AT&T and the other members of Telecommute America, available online at http://www.att.com/Telecommute_America.

16. For more information on anonymous remailers, consult http://www.anonymizer.com. Also see http://www.well.com/user/abacard/remail.html for a list of frequently asked questions about anonymous remailers. The list was created by Andre Bacard, author of *Computer Privacy Handbook* (Berkeley, Calif.: Peachpit Press, 1995).

17. Judge Alvarez, cited in Louis Henkin, Richard C. Pugh, Oscar Schachter, and Hans Smit, *International Law—Cases and Materials* (St. Paul, Minn.: West Publishing Co., 1980), 13.

18. See David R. Johnson and David G. Post, "Law and Borders," *Release 1.0* (Esther Dyson's monthly report), 19 June 1996, 1–30; and *Law and Borders: The Rise of Law in Cyberspace,* 48 Stanford L Rev, 1367 (1996), available online at http://www.cli.org/X0025_LBFIN.html.

19. See David R. Johnson and David G. Post's contribution to this volume for a discussion of national sovereignty under the pressure of global communications.

20. In the end, Worldcom outbid British Telecom, so the BT–MCI merger did not occur. Nevertheless, such international mergers are becoming increasing frequent and illustrate the globalization of the telecommunications industry.

21. "The Disappearing Taxpayer," *The Economist,* 31 May 1997, 15; "Disappearing Taxes—The Tap Runs Dry," *The Economist,* 31 May 1997, 21–23.

22. *Selected Tax Policy Implications of Global Electronic Commerce* (Washington, D.C.: U.S. Department of Treasury, Office of Tax Policy, November 1996).

23. Over the last two years, the G10 nations and members of the Organization for Economic Cooperation and Development (OECD) have held a number of meetings on taxation issues posed by electronic commerce. For instance, on 19–21 November 1997, the OECD held a conference in Turku, Finland, whose topic was "Dismantling the Barriers to Global Electronic Commerce." The organization is preparing for a ministerial meeting on the same topic, to be held in Canada in October 1998.

24. Jessica Mathews, "Power Shift," *Foreign Affairs,* January 1997, 50–66.

25. "The Future of Money" (an interview with Walter Wriston), *Wired,* October 1996, p. 140+, available online at http://www.wired.com/wired/4.10/features/wriston.html.

26. Alvin Toffler, *Power Shift—Knowledge, Wealth, and Violence at the Edge of the*

21st Century (New York: Bantam Books, 1991), 468.

27. This figure is based on 1993 and 1995 data on state and local government compiled by the U.S. Census Bureau and available online at http://www.census.gov/govs/www/apesloc.html.

28. See the National Performance Review online at http://www.npr.gov/accompli/index.html.

29. Details of the Bonn ministerial conference on Global Information Networks (6–8 July 1997) can be found online at http://www2.echo.lu/bonn/conference.html.

30. The ministers agreed to a communique, which is available online at http://www/insight.mcmaster.ca/org/efc/pages/doc/g7.html.

31. Admittedly, the Chinese Army later moved in, attacking and killing hundreds of students in Tiananmen Square, but they did so at night when it was difficult for the media to capture the event.

32. Greenpeace's Brent Spar Web page is available online at http://xs2.greenpeace.org/~comms/brent.

33. For more information on the Communications Decency Act and the Supreme Court decision overturning it, refer to http://www.ciec.org, the home page of the Citizens Internet Empowerment Coalition.

34. The recent "Internet Online Summit—Focus on Children," held 1–3 December 1997, highlighted the potential of these new filtering and rating systems. Details on the conference are available online at http://www.kidsonline.org.

35. Anderson, "In Search of the Perfect Market."

36. The Better Business Bureau can be found online at http://www.bbb.org. Web sites such as those run by CNET (http://www.cnet.com) or the Ziff-Davis Corporation (http://www.zdnet.com) provide invaluable comparisons of computers, software, and Internet service providers.

37. *Framework for Global Electronic Commerce* (Washington, D.C.: The White House, 1997), available online at http://www.ecommerce.gov.

38. Ibid.

39. Walter Wriston, lecture delivered to the Harvard Club, 28 May 1992; published as "The Nationhood Lectures: The Twilight of Sovereignty," *RSA Journal* (August/September 1992). Quotation is from page 567.

40. Information on the White House forum is available at http://www.whitehouse.gov/WH/EOP/OSTP/forum/html/gii-draft.html.

41. Stuart J. D. Schwartzstein, ed., *The Information Revolution and National Security: Dimensions and Directions* (Washington, D.C.: Center for Strategic and International Studies, 1996).

42. Kenneth G. Robinson, *Bits Across Borders: Policy Choices for International Multimedia and Digital Services,* a report of the second annual Aspen Institute Roundtable on International Telecommunications (Washington, D.C.: Aspen Institute, 1997). See also Kenneth G. Robinson, *Building a Global Information Society,* a report of the Aspen Institute Roundtable on International Telecommunications (Washington, D.C.: Aspen Institute, 1996). Additional information is available online at http://www.aspeninst.org/dir/polpro/CSP/AIRIT/AIRIT.html.

THE NEW "CIVIC VIRTUE" OF THE INTERNET

David R. Johnson

Co-Director, Cyberspace Law Institute
Director, The Aspen Institute Internet Policy Project

David G. Post

Co-Director, Cyberspace Law Institute
Associate Professor of Law, Temple University

A great deal of talk these days concerns "wrongful" conduct in cyberspace—rampant copyright infringement, easily accessible online gambling sites, widely disseminated pyramid schemes, and pornographic images available at the click of a mouse to any Net-savvy fourteen-year-old. What to do about all this wrongful conduct is unclear—it is, after all, hard to arrest an electron. Law enforcement (understood in the broadest sense to encompass both public and private law) is unusually problematic in the special environment of cyberspace; not only can it be difficult to locate an anonymous or pseudonymous Internet user within any specific territorial jurisdiction, but the global nature of the Internet decreases the likelihood that the parties to online disputes will be subject to control by the same territorial law enforcement entities.

These are serious enforcement issues, deserving serious attention. But even more important questions must first be considered: Who should *set* the rules that apply to this new global medium? What polity or polities should function as *sources* of legitimate and welfare-enhancing rules for conduct on the Internet? Who should become the *lawmakers* of cyberspace?

One obvious answer is that cyberspace should be controlled by those same territorial sovereigns who set the rules governing conduct offline. In this chapter, we argue that this most obvious answer may well be wrong. We question whether a governance system divided into territories demarcated by physical boundaries can achieve key governmental goals in an environment that decouples the effects of conduct from the physical location in which that conduct occurs.

This is certainly a disorienting and disturbing suggestion, and we do not make it lightly. After several millennia of experimentation, civilization has produced models of governance with which many people are—justifiably—rather pleased. And as the world nears the close of the twentieth century, territorial sovereigns, by and large (and with notable exceptions, to be sure) seem to be embracing democratic values that responsibly serve the interests of their citizens. Substantial discomfort can be expected to accompany any suggestion that existing governance mechanisms will not work well in the new online environment, and that the nature of governance and what we call "civic virtue" themselves may change in fundamental ways (at least as applied to online conduct that principally affects others engaged in online commerce and communities).

But new conceptualizations necessitated by the failure of traditional, geographically based governance mechanisms in the online context may well lead to the emergence of new means of producing a just ordering of human affairs online—means that may in turn lead to new and generalizable insights into what constitutes superior design in collective decision-making processes in other spheres as well. As the authors of this chapter have argued elsewhere,[1] the establishment of rules specifically designed to apply to online spaces, and the recognition of the legal and practical significance of the electronic boundaries that define, separate, and shield particular online spaces, provide the greatest hope for establishing an effective and legitimate governance system for the Internet.

This chapter, applying recent work involving the study of complex systems, develops our contention that allowing the Internet to evolve laws of its own (in a manner that does not use "representative democracy" of the type we value in the context of geographically defined sovereigns) will systematically produce a better means of finding optimal solutions to "collective-action" problems involving activities online.

Representative democracy is grounded in the notion that participation in deliberations on the public good both requires and leads to civic virtue. Men and women (whether acting as voters or representatives) are ennobled by the process of casting aside narrow, selfish, or factional interests and putting themselves in the special frame of mind known as "good citizenship."[2] Any scheme for governance of the Internet that is not grounded in representative democracy's traditional concepts of citizenship and civic virtue (which have historically been applied within geographically defined polities) must show itself to be superior to governance relying on "high-minded" public dialogue regarding policy issues and/or a system whereby citizens vote for representatives who can themselves engage in such deliberations.

A preview of our conclusions is in order at the outset: Rather than rely upon even the best of our democratic traditions to create a single set of top-down laws to impose on the Internet, would-be regulators of cyberspace should instead foster the emergence of diverse and contending rule sets that "pull and tug" against each other (and that help to recruit or discourage potential participants in particular online spaces) in order to allow an optimal overall combination of rules to arise. Rather than rely on the ability of citizens of the global electronic polity to debate thoughtfully in search of a *single, shared* vision of the common good, would-be architects of online governance systems should look for a form of civic virtue that can tolerate continuous conflict and can reside in the very architecture of a decentralized, diverse, complex adaptive system.

The best available solution to conflicts in individual goals and values regarding online conduct may be found by allowing individuals to join distinct, boundaried communities on the Internet, each with its own divergent set of rules, and by allowing those communities to deal with *external* pressures by devising their own mechanisms for filtering out unwelcome messages and with *internal* conflict by easing (or requiring) exit. Democratic debate and traditional legislative action may not, after all, be the best way to make the best public policy for the Internet. If we can preserve individual liberty to make educated and empowering choices among alternative online rule sets, our most thoughtful and high-minded collective-action option may be to abandon the process of elections and deliberations regarding some single best law to be imposed impartially on all from the top down. We may instead find a new form of civic virtue by allowing the governance of online actions to emerge "from the bottom up" as a result of the pull and tug between local online "jurisdictions" that do not attempt to act in a dispassionate or disinterested or "public-spirited" manner.

GOVERNANCE AS A SYSTEM-DESIGN PROBLEM

Imagine designing a new governance system from scratch for a particular population. Central to the task would be the creation of a set of processes and institutions enabling citizens to seek the collective good. Designers of any system of governance need to define what is and is not "wrongful," create enforceable rules to govern conduct, and set up mechanisms to enforce those rules. They need, in short, to solve the ever-present problem(s) of collective action.

To survive and to produce sound policies, the proposed mechanism of governance would need, substantially, to satisfy two key design constraints. The first constraint, *legitimacy*, serves to limit a governing authority's right to coerce its citizens—and thereby helps to assure long-term support. Because a major function of governance is to prohibit wrongful self-interested conduct, governance necessarily involves an exercise of coercive authority; it is precisely the prospect of individual "defection" from agreed-upon rules that calls for governance in the first place, and it is to the common good to have cooperative rules enforced against those who would defect from those rules. But to limit the tyrannical exercise of coercive power, and to keep it from becoming oppressive, some principle along the lines of "consent of the governed" must be adopted: Those whose conduct is to be controlled by particular law-making exercises must have some "voice" (directly, or through some form of representation) in determining the substance of the laws.

The second design constraint, *internalization*, limits a governing authority's ability to make laws whose effects "spill over" onto those outside its "territory." Because a geographic territory's laws may have large-scale effects, some of the people affected by the actions of its citizens may be located outside the boundaries of that territory. For example, to use a common illustration, sovereign X's rule regarding factory emissions may, because of the ability of those emissions to cross geographic boundaries, affect the well-being of individuals living within the jurisdiction of sovereigns Y, Z, and so on. Governance mechanisms must limit this problem of "spillover" if they are to produce general welfare-enhancing rules.[3] This is because the presence of substantial spillovers (or *externalities*) tends to diminish one's confidence that rules adopted by individual sovereigns will be welfare-enhancing *in the aggregate*, for it is only to be expected that rules with negative external effects (i.e., rules whose costs are largely borne by outsiders) will be produced at the expense of rules with positive external effects (rules whose benefits are largely realized by outsiders). To protect against substantial negative effects of spillover, then, requires the adoption of a second principle: Those who feel the effects of conduct regulated by particular rules should, to a substantial degree, have a voice in determining the substantive content of the rules.

These two design goals—that both those who are *controlled by* and those who are *affected by* particular law-making exercises should have a voice in determining the substantive content of those laws—define two sets of individuals with a "stake" in the law-making process. A well-designed governance system, we assert, as have many before us, should give those two sets of individuals the predominant voice in the design of those laws.

Legitimacy and Internalization in the Real World: The Roles of Physical Clustering and Geographically Defined Citizenship

In the "real world"—the world of atoms—the usual system of law-making sovereignty is generally defined in geographical terms. That is, both the power and the right to enact and enforce laws are lodged with sovereigns whose domain of authority is circumscribed in *territorial* terms—applicable within a particular geographic area to persons (real or fictional), events, and conduct located there.[4] Defining sovereignty in terms of geography means that the sovereign can legitimately exercise coercive power only over those individuals bearing some relationship to the particular geographical territory over which the sovereign has control.

In the case of designing a government for a "real" world of geographic sovereignty, the legitimacy-related design goal can be satisfied by incorporating a design element we might call *geographically defined citizenship*: Individuals who bear some relationship to the geographical territory over which the sovereign exercises control should have a voice in the sovereign's exercise of that law-making power. In this way, the set of individuals who have a stake in the content of the sovereign's laws arising from the sovereign's right and ability to exert coercive power over them corresponds to the set of persons who, through the constitution of law-making institutions, control the exercise of that power.

If the effects of conduct taking place at a particular location are felt primarily by those individuals located geographically at or near that location, then the second design goal—internalization—can also be satisfied by defining the "real-world" set of lawmakers in geographic terms. Where this assumption of *physical clustering* holds true, the set of individuals collectively deciding the rules applicable to particular conduct—the individuals located within sovereign X's boundaries—will substantially overlap the set of those individuals whose well-being is primarily *affected* by those rules, because those latter individuals are also predominantly located within sovereign X's boundaries.

Geographical clustering of the effects of physical conduct is thus a sufficient condition for territorially defined citizenship simultaneously to serve *both* of the basic goals of well-designed governance. Of course this is no accident. Both the ability to ascertain the will of a proximate people and the ability to affect the welfare of those people by means of enforceable rules arise traditionally from communications technologies that operate best at close range and on enforcement by means of physical forces that work best within shorter distances. The world in which the impact of governmental action damps down or attenuates over distance is also a world in which individual actions affect most intensely those who are physically closest to the actor.

Where the assumptions of physical clustering and geographically defined citizenship hold, the act of constituting authoritative sets of lawmakers geographically allows reasonable certainty that the two key design goals for good governance will be met. In this setting, the major concerns for enhancing "civic virtue" will relate to the quality of the conversation among those geographically defined citizens, the thoughtfulness of representatives regarding the "public good" as defined with reference to this geographically defined "public," and, perhaps, some thought about the optimal size of geographic territories that can appropriately be brought under a single government's rule.[5] But what of the goals of legitimacy and internalization as applied to the governance of cyberspace, where the effect of conduct is *not* contained by physical clustering? Does geographically defined governance make sense for such a realm?

Legitimacy and Internalization in Cyberspace: The Absence of Physical Clustering

Throughout most of human history, human interaction has been governed by laws based on geographically defined citizenship and physical clustering; rules applicable to conduct in, say, a medieval manor or a tribal village had little effect on individuals physically located elsewhere. But it is already a commonplace to observe that this state of affairs has begun to crumble in recent years as a result of the proliferation of cross-border externalities of all kinds. In an increasingly interconnected world, conduct occurring "there" (wherever "there" might be) increasingly affects those located "here"; yet people "here" who are affected by that conduct may have no voice in whether such conduct may lawfully occur, because that decision is left to the citizens of "there."

Although people still live in geographically defined territories, cyberspace has accelerated humanity's transition to a world in which physical clustering virtually disappears, at least with respect to the kinds of activities typical to an online environment.[6] Cyberspace does not merely weaken the physical clustering assumption (that conduct taking place at a particular geographical location primarily affects persons at or near that physical location); cyberspace renders the assumption virtually unintelligible. Nor does cyberspace merely weaken geographical boundaries, it obliterates them entirely (at least in cyberspace), because geographical location itself is both indeterminate and irrelevant for transactions on the Internet.

Location is *indeterminate* because no necessary relationship exists between electronic addressing—such as Internet Protocol addresses, domain names, and e-mail addresses—and the location of the addressee (machine or user) in physical space.[7] It is, perhaps, conceivable that the entire Internet could be redesigned in some way to alter addressing functions so as to retain, or even emphasize, their connection to geographical reality.[8] But the absence of any connection to geographic location is a fundamental and immutable characteristic of other network interactions; distributed databases (such as Usenet newsgroups), for example, have no single place of existence at all, but are aggregates of information stored on a large (and constantly changing) number of individual machines at any time.[9]

Location is also *irrelevant* in cyberspace in the sense that network servers and online addressees are equally accessible from everywhere. Any Web site in any odd corner of the network can be accessed with essentially equivalent transmission speed and message quality from any other corner of the network, which means that the effects of whatever information is available at a given site are felt simultaneously and equally in all jurisdictions, independent of their "distance" from one another. This is a function of the speed at which information travels (and "information," strings of bits, is all that *does* travel in cyberspace) and of the digital character of that information, which does not decay as a function of time and distance.

If physical clustering is not thus a valid assumption with regard to activities on the Internet, important questions arise with regard to governance and cyberspace: Is physical clustering a *necessary* condition for the use of geographically defined territories to achieve the two basic design goals of legitimacy and internalization in governance? If physical clustering is absent, must we abandon geographically defined governance structures in order to serve those key goals? While cyberspace's "inhabitants" have physical bodies that reside in geographically defined territories, the online world itself exists without physical clustering of effects (i.e., it is a world in which the effects of particular actions, as well as the effects of the rules that regulate them, are randomly distributed with respect to geographic location). Lacking the organization of effects provided by physical clustering, can geographically defined citizenship (and rule-making) simultaneously serve the goals of legitimacy and internalization in such a space as cyberspace? We believe that they cannot.

To illustrate, consider a simple hypothetical scenario: Residents of one country—say France—place a World Wide Web page on a server in that jurisdiction. The Web page displays content created by residents of a different jurisdiction—say the United States—in a manner (a) consistent with French copyright law but (b) inconsistent with U.S. copyright law.[10] Whose law applies to this conduct? Applying French law in this case appears to comport with design goal #1 (legitimacy), inasmuch as the offending (and regulated) conduct takes place within French territory. But it contravenes design goal #2 (internalization) inasmuch as the rule primarily affects the content's authors, who are located in the United States. Conversely, application of U.S. law comports with design goal #2, inasmuch as the authors of the content reside in U.S. territory, but violates design goal #1 because the French actors are then bound by a law they had no voice in making. The same dilemma arises in reference to any action on the Internet that involves conduct viewed differently by differing sovereigns (trademark violations, publication of "offensive" content, defamation, and so on), whenever the originating parties and those affected by their acts reside in different countries. The dilemma is not solved whether sovereigns opt to impose law *territorially* (and thereby contravene the principle that individuals should have a voice in rules that affect them) or *extraterritorially* (and thereby contravene the principle that individuals should have a voice in rules that are applied to them).

As a result of an increasingly interconnected world, dilemmas of this sort were already becoming more frequent even before the invention of the Internet. The recent—and ongoing—explosion of the World Wide Web, however, has brought the problem to the forefront: How can the principles of legitimacy and internalization be substantially satisfied in a bit-based world in which the inherent overlap of control and effect accomplished by physical clustering—an atom-based phenomenon—can no longer be assumed?

CLUSTERING AND RULE-MAKING IN COMPLEX SYSTEMS

To study the implications of a world in which the effects of conduct extend beyond geographical boundaries ("spilling over" into other jurisdictions) and participation in rule-making is decoupled from the effects of such rules, we have created a computer-based complex system and studied its behavior under various circumstances.[11]

Our computer-based complex system is based on seminal research conducted by Stuart Kauffman and his colleagues at the Santa Fe Institute in New Mexico.[12] Kauffman's original system can be understood in terms of a collection of individual elements—light bulbs, say— each of which can be "on" or "off" (i.e., each of which may be in one of two possible "states"). Each individual element has a "fitness" rating (we could say "happiness" or "utility") that is partially determined by its own state (on/off); that is, some light bulbs "prefer" to be on, others "prefer" to be off. In addition, however, each light bulb's fitness is also a function of the on/off state of some number of other light bulbs; that is, spillover effects exist by which the state of any particular element affects the fitness of many other elements and the fitness of any particular element is affected by the state of many other elements.

Suppose we are looking for the particular configuration of on/off settings for all light bulbs that produces the highest aggregate fitness for the system as a whole. If we simply try to place each light bulb in its individually "preferred" on/off state, we run into immediate trouble, because the interests of the individual light bulbs conflict; for example, one bulb's preferred state may negatively affect the fitness of large numbers of others. Next we could try, systematically, to examine all possible configurations of the light bulbs (all combinations and permutations of on/off settings for the entire matrix) to find the best configuration (i.e., the one producing the highest aggregate fitness). But this procedure is computationally intractable; with even a small system of, say, 100 light bulbs, we would have to examine 2^{100} different configurations. (The many different possible combinations of interdependent states create what Kauffman calls a "rugged" fitness landscape—one that produces many peaks, foothills, valleys, and chasms, and one that (1) does not have a reliable or smooth "uphill" direction, and (2) is simply too large to explore fully by trudging one step at a time across the combinations of settings that produce, at any point, its topographic "height.")

We could, in desperation, begin to switch randomly chosen light bulbs from one state to another and observe whether the change increases, or decreases, the overall (aggregate) fitness of the system. But, as Kauffman and others have demonstrated, this approach—this step-by-step "algorithm" for searching out the best "policy" for attaining the fitness of the matrix as a whole—often gets stuck at a low level of overall fitness; whenever the system arrives, randomly, at the top of a low foothill on the fitness landscape, it cannot dislodge itself because every possible one-step change in state leads the overall fitness (temporarily) downward off the hill.

Kauffman's experiments with these models have demonstrated the effectiveness of one particular algorithm for finding high aggregate fitness for complex systems, one that mediates between the local ("selfish") interests of the individual element (e.g., light bulb) and the global ("public") interests of the total system. To use Kauffman's approach, we begin by dividing the entire population of light bulbs into discrete "patches"—groups of neighboring elements. (As we will explain in more detail later in this chapter, the size and character of these patches do have an important impact. In his own experiments, Kauffman selected patch sizes at random and examined the results). Now, as we change the state of a randomly chosen light bulb, we monitor the effect of that switch on the aggregate fitness of that bulb's patch. We then judge any particular "move" by assessing only the resulting well-being of the light bulb's patch—not the impact on the bulb itself and not the impact on the matrix as a whole. That is, if the move causes patch fitness to decline, we return the light bulb to its initial state, even if the move would have benefited either or both the individual and the matrix as a whole; conversely, if the move causes patch fitness to increase, the change of state is allowed to stand even if the move disadvantages the individual and/or the matrix as a whole. As we continue to switch randomly selected bulbs in this way, the overall fitness of the matrix increases—to values higher than those achievable with other methods.

Kauffman has demonstrated that allowing patches to use this method to optimize their internal fitness is a highly effective way to find a high aggregate fitness for the system as a whole (and, of course, for the "average" individual element). The algorithm works because it allows "selfish" decisions by local patches, configurations that can drive the fitness of the overall matrix temporarily downhill. (This effect stems from spillover impacts across patch boundaries.) Over time, however, these selfish patch decisions help drive the system as a whole to positions of higher overall fitness (as all patches continue to seek optimization within the context of other patches' "decisions"). Kauffman's patches work better than algorithms that confirm moves rewarding only the individual or the system as a whole. And they work even though—indeed, *because*—some of the effects of the patches' decisions fall on "neighbors" who are not "voting" members of the patch. As should be apparent, Kauffman's work thus suggests that—in the context of complex systems with many elements that exhibit many conflicting goals—algorithms that define the problem in terms of finding moves that benefit either individuals or the "public" as a whole may not be optimal. And, as we will discuss at greater length, Kauffman's work shows that some degree of spillover (and its resulting "illegitimacy") may not be a bad thing.

That such a system of decision-making by patches that pull and tug against each other is apparently the most effective way to find the highest aggregate fitness for an entire collection of individuals with conflicting goals demonstrates the value of a primitive kind of decentralized federalism. It suggests that the welfare of all may, on average, be maximized not by allowing each individual to seek its own good, nor by deciding centrally what appears to be best for the whole. Optimal solutions may come (in a complex-systems context) from a particular structure that seems, superficially, to make "wrong" collective-action choices from the perspectives of both the entire polity and some individuals negatively affected by those decisions. This is because complex systems produce rugged fitness landscapes, in which paths to an optimal set of results or policies may lead "downhill" from a suboptimal (but locally highest) foothill.[13]

We believe that, as a highly abstract representation, this model captures certain essential features of the existing international legal order. In that context, the system's elements are not light bulbs but a large number of individuals, each of whom derives some subjective happiness, or utility, as a consequence of (1) being permitted or (0) not being permitted to undertake a particular action.[14] Individuals' personal utility is a function not only of their own states (act/don't act), but also of the states (actions) of many other individuals; that is, utility is a function both of whether the individual is permitted to take an action that affects others and whether neighboring individuals are permitted to take actions that affect the individual (and others). Kauffman's "patches" are, in effect, territorially local sovereign political groups; each group decides whether conduct by its individual group members will, or will not, be permitted, and each group makes that decision on the basis of the aggregate well-being of its own members, without taking into account the effect of that conduct on persons outside the group.

If we want to apply the lessons from Kauffman's model to cyberspace, how should we organize and implement this decentralized, "federalist" decision-making algorithm? The decision of how to divide the online population into "patches" is critical. Must the patches somehow be defined in terms of *geographical* "neighborhoods"? If so, how can "patches" of decision-makers be created in a online world in which effects (and involvement in rule-making) don't necessarily cluster geographically? We built a version of Kauffman's model in an attempt to answer the following question: How much does the effectiveness of this patching algorithm in a complex-systems model depend upon the overlap between the set of those whose conduct is regulated by a given patch's rules and the set of those who are affected by the impact (spillover effects) of the actions permitted by those rules? We have returned, in other words, to the original question—whether physical clustering is a necessary prerequisite for the use of geographic sovereignty as the basis for governance of online activities—but we can now analyze that question in terms of the behavior of Kauffman's computer-based complex systems, under carefully controlled conditions.

In Kauffman's original model, spillovers and patch membership were both determined by a light bulb's physical location within the overall matrix—i.e., geographically defined "citizenship." Thus, Kauffman's patches inevitably consisted to a substantial degree of groups of light bulbs whose fitness was substantially affected by the state (action) of other patch members. We asked: Suppose we systematically unhook the "spillover sets" (the elements that affect one another's well-being) and what we can call the "political patches" (the elements that collectively decide whether particular conduct is permissible). That is, what if, at one extreme, we allow light bulbs to affect the fitness only of other light bulbs who cannot "vote" on those moves (whose "fitness" is not counted to determine if the "patch" is better off)? And what if, at the other extreme, we only allow light bulbs to affect the fitness of other bulbs that are members of the same political patch, so that all decisions on individual moves are made only by assessing the well-being of the bulb making the move and the other bulbs affected by those moves? We asked: Will the patching algorithm still work to maximize overall system well-being when the "internalization" (spillover) and "legitimacy" dials are twisted to one extreme or the other?

Our results were quite striking. When we set up the system so that bulbs only affect others who can vote to roll back their moves, we got lower overall fitness results. When we set up the system so there was no connection between those who voted and those affected by actions permitted by such votes, we also got lower aggregate fitness results. "Congruence"—the amount of overlap between the effects of individual elements' actions and "political" patch membership—turns out to be a critical determinant of the patching algorithm's success. Systems that are set up with very low congruence (that is, the effects of an individual's change of state are felt primarily by elements outside its decision-making unit) do systematically *worse* at solving the collective-action problem of finding a high overall fitness score (maximizing average and aggregate "utility," considering the state of all elements). Perhaps even more interesting, however, is our finding that too much "congruence" also makes patching less effective; if an individual's conduct affects *only* the other members of its decision-making group, then dividing the system into patches does not effectively drive the overall matrix towards a better solution—because there is no way for the patch to push the overall matrix down a hill in the overall "fitness space" and thus no way the matrix can climb up a ridge to a higher hill. Thus, in light of the benefits of "patching," neither perfect "internalization" nor perfect "legitimacy" are optimal for the governance of complex systems. Effects and rule-making authority need to be connected—but only to an optimal degree. (We found the optimal level at approximately eighty to ninety percent overlap, or congruence, in our system, given the particular spillover settings and matrix size we used in our experiments.)

Our computer-based complex system and Kauffman's groundbreaking work thus provide strong evidence that the best way to solve the complex problems of collective action by interdependent groups with conflicting goals is to cut polities up into smaller "patches" that are defined in a way that preserves some optimal degree (neither zero nor 100 percent; approximately eighty percent, in our findings) of congruence, or overlap, between those who are affected by particular rules and those with a voice in setting those rules. A world of *geographically* defined decision-making patches makes sense as a means of solving the problem of finding optimal rules, but *only* if the effects of individual conduct are felt primarily within those *same* geographical boundaries, i.e., only if there is a relatively small (approximately twenty percent) degree of cross-border spillover. The physical clustering assumption thus may not only be a sufficient condition for the effectiveness of geographically defined governance, it appears to be a *necessary* condition if we want governance to maximize utility in aggregate.[15] But because physical clustering is a condition that does not hold for most online activities, we need to look to other mechanisms that can, for cyberspace, preserve (or, more accurately, reestablish) an optimal degree of congruence.

REESTABLISHING CONGRUENCE IN
CYBERSPACE GOVERNANCE

So far this chapter has examined governance as a design problem substantially constrained by the two key goals of achieving substantial legitimacy and internalization of spillovers. The time-honored design solution provided by the physical clustering of effects in the "real" world of geographically defined citizenship seems inadequate for solving the governance problem in the online world, where the physical clustering of effects can no longer be taken for granted. This has created a seemingly intractable dilemma for territorial governments.

The behavior of computer-based, complex-system models helps us to understand and analyze both the new phenomena presented by cyberspace and the initial reactions of territorial governments in response to these phenomena. The Internet, we observe, dramatically reduces the "congruence" between rule-making and spillover impact sets that otherwise naturally exists in the real, atom-based, world by allowing the actions of an individual located just about anywhere on earth (whose conduct is now regulated by territorially local laws) to affect any number of others located just about anywhere. Now that spillovers no longer fall predominantly on individuals belonging to the same geographically defined patch, rule-making decisions made by these patches—sovereign states—are less likely to find the highest peaks on the global policy fitness landscape. A central question for Internet governance, then, is: How can an optimal level of "congruence" be reestablished in the online world?

Suboptimal Ways to Reestablish Congruence
A number of remedies for repairing a loss of congruence within the Internet are already being advanced. Each of them, however, has significant limitations or negative consequences:

1. *Treat the entire system as a single patch.* To eliminate low patch/spillover overlap in any system, all external spillover effects could be internalized by treating all individuals as members of a single, system-wide patch. This "single patch" strategy is reflected in increasingly frequent calls for a global governance mechanism for the Internet to achieve a "harmonization" of substantive rules regarding particular activities in cyberspace (and thereby take into account the geographical-

boundary–destroying character of the Internet).[16] Global harmonization may indeed remove some of the negative effects of spillovers. But this strategy also eliminates the benefits that the decentralized patching algorithm might otherwise provide. A single-patch (harmonized) system will tend to get stuck on low local optima because decisions by subsidiary patches cannot override the central consensus, and cannot thereby drive the matrix towards a better solution. A single system of global governance for the Internet might be legitimate (if all participants had a say) and would necessarily internalize all costs and benefits within a single decision-making entity. But it would still not be the best algorithm for collective action, because it could not make use of the benefits of federalism—the ability of local experiments to cause reactions and adjustments by adversely affected "neighbors," creating a pull and tug among conflicting rule sets that ultimately causes the overall matrix to achieve a better solution.

2. *Recouple spillover sets and patch membership by filtering spillovers so that they fall more clearly within geographic patch boundaries.* If "political patch" boundaries are regarded as geographically fixed, a recoupling of spillover effects and patch boundaries might be achieved by controlling spillover effects at those geographic boundaries. Filtering spillovers so that they fall more clearly within geographic borders—that is, interposing existing geopolitical patch boundaries on the flow of information across the network so as to eliminate unwelcome effects spilling across those boundaries—is a strategy used by many territorial governments. The government of Singapore, for example, has at times attempted to control World Wide Web content accessible to its citizens by means of a "proxy server" system that permits access from within Singapore only to previously downloaded copies of "approved" Web pages.[17] German authorities try to disable access by German residents to certain global Usenet newsgroups deemed pornographic.[18]

Implementation of geographically based spillover-filtering systems in cyberspace is likely to be costly in the extreme and quite possibly futile, at least under cyberspace's current network architecture, which allows the routing of messages without reference to locational information.[19] More importantly—the ultimate futility of such measures aside—this strategy is counterproductive, as it has as its aim the elimination of interpatch spillover effects that are, from other perspectives, the new medium's most obvious strengths. Converting the global marketplace into a series of geographically defined local flea markets solves the "excess spillover" problem, but only by denying everyone the chance to participate in global electronic commerce, which inherently consists of widely scattered spillover sets. In addition, this "solution" tends, like the harmonization approach, to create isolated, totally congruent patches, thereby reducing system search efficiency (losing the benefits of patching) and, in effect, destroying the Internet in order to save it.

3. *Recouple spillover sets and patch membership by redrawing geographic political patch boundaries so that they encompass foreign sources of spillovers.* If political law-making and law-enforcing boundaries are not viewed as fixed, then patch boundaries themselves—in the form of the legally operative borders of nation-states—might be adjusted to track spillover effects. As in our earlier example of a hypothetical U.S./France dispute over copyright law, we could extend the power of local governments to cover any participant in an online space who has any impact on the local territory (whether or not "targeted"). But this would not repair congruence fully or symmetrically. Allowing Germany, for example, to set rules applicable to everyone whose actions in an online forum affect any German citizen checks the "spillover" onto German interests, but disserves the goal of legitimacy because "foreign" participants in such online spaces do not have a say in establishing German law. Extending the reach of local jurisdictions can check spillovers, but, absent more radical changes regarding participation in local law-making, the natural two-sided "congruence" found in geographically based governance of the tangible world is not repaired. In addition, conflicts among the rules of local jurisdictions inevitably subject individual actors to multiple, inconsistent, purportedly equally binding rules of law.

This third category presents an option all too popular with local governments and is most obviously illustrated by attempts by existing sovereigns to extend their authority to encompass activities—wherever located—whose effects spill into their jurisdictions by asserting a "jurisdiction to prescribe" in respect to outside-the-boundary activities. An example is the attempt by Minnesota to regulate gambling that occurs on a foreign Web page because it can be accessed and "brought into" the state by a local resident.[20] In this case, a single "patch" is attempting to govern the actions of those outside of its borders when those actions have, in the view of the local patch members, a detrimental effect on the fitness/happiness of the patch's citizenry. The local authority uses local effects as the basis for asserting its "long-arm" jurisdiction and applying its law.

While redefining patch boundaries by expanding a geographic patch's "jurisdiction to prescribe" does achieve a degree of recoupling, it does so only asymmetrically. Patching performs two separate functions: (1) patches are loci of decision-making processes, defining the members of the set whose preferences count in regard to determining the desirability of particular moves, and (2) patches are enforcement devices, empowered to "roll back" those actions/changes of which patch members collectively disapprove. Extending a geographical patch's jurisdiction to prescribe adjusts that patch's boundary only for the latter (enforcement) purpose; patch boundaries are extended only for purposes of exercising "vetoes" on actions by individuals outside the patch boundary, not for granting those individuals membership in the patch itself (i.e., those individuals are not permitted to participate in the determination of the acceptability of particular changes). In such a case, the patch boundary is thus made selectively permeable, a kind of one-way valve that grants only partial patch membership to those whose activities spill into its jurisdiction. This asymmetry can be expected to encourage strategic behavior on the part of the patch members that systematically disserves the liberty interests of external actors. Extraterritorial application of patch decisions not only threatens core "legitimacy" goals, it gives individual patches an *incentive* to attempt to impose regulatory burdens on those who cannot affect decision-making regarding the scope of those burdens—to export regulatory costs to individuals lacking a voice.[21]

A Better Way to Reestablish Congruence

We are aware of only one way to repair the needed level of congruence in the online world without eliminating the virtues of federalism implicit in patching or otherwise harming legitimacy and internalization goals. That way is to allocate decision-making regarding the rules applicable to particular areas of the online world to those people who are most affected by such activities—the system operator and the users who actually "inhabit" the online spaces in question. These "netizens" are the people for whom the rules regarding action in this online space have the greatest significance—for whom the rules are, in the most meaningful (and non-geographical) sense, a "local" ordinance. Actions in this space may have some "spillover" effects on other real or virtual places. But, with rare exceptions, such spillovers are less important than the impact of the rules on those who choose to participate directly in such online space(s).

Insofar as online activities involve communications of information, and insofar as the areas in which such communications take place are separated by meaningful boundaries—login codes, habits of users who visit some spaces and not others, filters that screen out incoming messages, and so on—the online world is building a non-physical type of "clustering" of effects and controls.[22] What is said in a Usenet newsgroup I never visit is less likely to have an impact on me—though it may occasionally "spill over" in various ways—than what is done in the online spaces I do choose to frequent. Rules designed to govern "conduct" on the Internet most directly affect those who take part actively in the online spaces where the rules apply. Thus, congruence between those whose actions are regulated, and those who are affected by those actions, can be "naturally" reestablished for cyberspace by respecting the natural electronic boundaries (filters and other separations of online spaces) that accomplish, for this new cyberspace, what physical separation and the attenuation of impacts and controls over distance have always accomplished for the geographical world.

We are mindful that some online activities have serious impact on those who are not participants in the online spaces whose rules permit the activities to occur. But there are long-distance impact exceptions that prove the rule (and justify self-defensive measures by a remote target) in the real world as well. In the general case of online spillovers, such as negative effects from offending messages, the ability to construct software filters that eliminate messages from specific sources should go far towards allowing any particular online group to avoid noxious spillover from another group that has differing views about what should be permitted online. Moreover, we must remember that the optimal level of spillover is not zero. We will learn a great deal, collectively, from the pull and tug among differing rule sets that contend for favor online—in part as a result of actions taken by differing groups to defend themselves against the negative externalities created by others with differing utility functions and/or political views.

Some Examples

Consider the problem posed by "spam"—defined generally as unsolicited commercial e-mail sent in bulk to many unwilling recipients. This practice poses two different types of challenges for Internet governance: (1) how to decide which spam is wrongful, and (2) how to enforce any such rule. If geographically based governments attempt to pass laws against spam (and the U.S. Congress is considering several bills right now), they may succeed only in driving prohibited practices offshore. If they attempt to extend their jurisdictions to cover any source of an unwelcome message received locally, the end result may be doctrines that significantly constrain the free flow of information on the Internet, that create substantial conflicts between local jurisdictions, and that fail to embody the symmetry (with regard to participation by the regulated in rule-making) implicit in the notion of legitimacy. Moreover, given the time it takes to pass laws and the difficulties in formulating authoritative texts to deal with fluid technical situations, any rules produced may quickly become outmoded as e-mail adds audio and video capability, as new filtering tools become available, and as messages begin to be exchanged among physical devices as well as human beings.

An alternative solution is to allow each online space to develop a set of rules of its own regarding both what messages to allow into local mailboxes and what conduct (in sending mail to others inside or outside the system) is permissible. Some online venues composed of those who hate getting spam will quickly adopt a rule prohibiting such conduct, on pain of banishment. (And they may, in some cases, expand the definition of the prohibited conduct to include non-commercial messages.) The sysops of those spaces will also try to establish effective filters against unwanted messages from outside, saving their members the time and effort involved in constructing personal barriers. In contrast, more "liberal" spaces may not bother to construct filters or, indeed, may tolerate spamming by members. A "spam haven" may evolve to expressly cater to those who send unrequested commercial e-mail for profit. But, from the perspective of remote victims, such havens may be easier to detect and filter out than a population of spammers randomly distributed across cyberspace domains. The spam havens may, to be sure, develop technology and practices designed to avoid the filters. But those who want to eliminate spam may also escalate their technological weapons and, in an extreme case, might band together to eliminate all routing of messages from the offending domain to their own areas of the Internet.[23]

This "pull and tug" of conflicting policies may lead to a complex de facto compromise based on the ability to attach labels to allow each side to deal only with others who follow policies acceptable to it. It will, in any event, surely allow the development of policies that (1) closely reflect the wishes of the users most affected (those who continue to frequent any particular online space because they endorse its local rules), (2) are capable of evolving rapidly in response to changes in underlying circumstances, (3) do not inherently (or de jure) unfairly impose one population's views of sound policy on another population whose actions do not affect the first, and (4) even allow a single individual to achieve a subtle mix of policies by means of spending differing portions of time in differing online spaces with differing policies. The result will not only achieve internalization goals (because it minimizes spillovers on those who find such spillover most noxious), achieve legitimacy goals (because it gives most say to those whose conduct is regulated by particular rules), and approach optimization (because its algorithm allows the kind of experimentation that leads more quickly to a high peak in policy space, even when perturbed by changing underlying circumstances), but it will also be personally empowering (because it allows individuals to decide whether and how to subject themselves to multiple differing rule sets.)

Spamming is a type of conduct that a disapproving "jurisdiction" can substantially reduce by means of filters. Can this decentralized model be extended to cover other types of actions whose impacts cannot so easily be filtered out? Consider Internet copyright rules, which affect authors by determining what other users of an online space may do with copies of the materials originating in that space, or defamation rules, which affect the reputations of those who may not frequent the online space where the defamatory comments are published. Even in these cases, diverse inconsistent rule sets could develop in a way that better serves the collective interest than traditional "top-down" democratic governance.

In the copyright case, areas liberally defining "fair use" (or, indeed, eliminating any prohibition at all against copying and subsequent distribution of an online author's works) would attract those who want to be free to reuse materials they find online and who would be willing to allow their own postings to be subject to such "liberal" copyright rules. (We are not here considering unauthorized "leakage" across boundaries but, instead, the various rules that might be applicable to texts originally posted with authorization in a particular online space with any particular set of rules regarding subsequent copying of such postings.) What we could expect, ultimately, is a sorting out of authors and readers and works into online spaces with rules that fit the combined preferences of specific groups of participants. Restrictive regimes will drive away (or expel, for rule violations) "liberally" minded readers. Liberal regimes will drive away authors who favor restrictive policies. And any effort on the part of either type of online "patch" to export costs onto the other will be met by retaliation in some form or other (such as rejection of visitors originating from, or downloads destined to, areas known to support disapproved policies). We end up with something that looks more like "foreign policy"—the familiar "pull and tug" among discrete patches—than representative democracy. But it might well work better, for all concerned, because it offers a diversity of differing rule sets as it preserves (1) incentives for those authors who need it (because they will practice their art only in areas that protect copyrights and prevent leakage) and (2) the free flow of information for those readers and authors who expect to prosper under more liberal rules.

The problem of online defamation, too, might be dealt with more successfully by a decentralized, emergent model of law-making. Assume that various people have thinner or thicker skins and worry to a greater or lesser degree about the free flow of robust discussion. Some will favor online areas that strictly limit apparently unreliable and derogatory comments. Some will favor areas that make no attempt to regulate false and damaging comments. Of course, a participant in the "defamation haven" might speak ill (and falsely) of an individual who never visits such dens of iniquity. Let's suppose the victim heard about it and that the comment had an actual substantial impact on the victim's reputation. If that occurred, and if the rule against defamation was taken seriously by the victim's own online venue (or local geographical sovereign), then the victim's sysop (or state) might be expected to seek to punish the offender—to prohibit messages or visits from the offending party or to seek to extract a remedy from the offending party by some means. An ugly online "war" might develop—but (assuming the victim's protective jurisdiction lacks physical control over the perpetrator and has no extradition power) its only casualties would be electronic messages. Perhaps a peace treaty among sysops might eventually provide that any victim of allegedly false and defamatory speech must be given an opportunity promptly to respond within the online context of the original message. Or perhaps some "defamation havens" would simply lose their power to inflict harms on reputation because (1) most readers wouldn't choose to go there, and (2) the very lack of any ability to bring a defamation action against speech originating in such fora would be known to attract just those persons interested in making false and unreliable statements, thereby automatically reducing the perceived reliability of messages originating there and thus lessening their negative impact. The overall, complex result is likely to be a state of affairs in which the personal preferences of actors and victims, regarding the vigor with which reliability is policed and reputational harm is remedied, more closely match the rules of the spaces where they spend their time.

Of course, autonomous online decision-making could allow some online spaces to develop rules that allow small groups to take actions that threaten the vital interests of "foreigners." The virtual or geographically based governments of those affected foreigners may then feel the need to protect their own "local" populations from such adverse spillover effects. If an online forum is used to plot violence against a particular country, that country might be justified in declaring war against the online upstart, wherever it happens to be based. Real-world governments and online governors will, of course, always need to protect their local populations against threats that emanate from "foreign" sources—and they will use whatever "force" they have at their disposal to do so in appropriate cases. But online areas that adopt rules allowing actions that primarily affect only willing participants, that reduce external spillovers to modest levels, and that are populated by users whose decisions set rules appropriate for such online spaces, are entitled to a certain amount of "comity"—the use of the contract enforcement mechanisms of real-world (and virtual) governments to assure respect for and the security of their virtual boundaries. Most importantly, geographically based governments can and should begin to pay attention to the possibility that the tendency of the Internet to break down geographic borders and eliminate physical clustering of effects requires a whole new perspective on how to measure the virtues of any particular governance mechanism applicable to activities on the Net.

CONGRUENCE, CYBERSPACE, AND CIVIC VIRTUE

We think that the most obvious path to reestablishing an optimal amount of legitimacy and internalization in cyberspace, while taking advantage of the virtues of federalism and of limited spillovers from local political patches, is to free cyberspace altogether from the notion that rules must be made (for online spaces) by institutions based on geographical sovereignty. To the contrary, the best "collective-action" results for cyberspace will be achieved by treating each separate online location as a distinct, largely self-governing place, with its own rules governing actions that primarily affect its own participants. (Those rules may be made in the first instance by system operators, but they will be ratified, in effect, by individual users' decisions to frequent the online spaces they find empowering.)

If rule-making is allocated to online groups in this way, other basic concepts will also need to be rethought, concepts that underlie notions of "civic virtue" in the context of traditional representative democracy and responsive geographic governance. Citizens of territorial democracies, for example, are accustomed to the idea that selection of representatives from a large territory can reduce the risks of factions, and that the number of representatives drawn from particular geographic regions must be set so as to allow constructive conversation in a real legislative chamber.[24] This may not work well in the context of online governance, because there can be no neat sorting of one-citizen, one-vote in cyberspace and because the "territory" that needs to be represented in the rule formulation process may be very large. Indeed, the search for ways to reestablish "congruence" (and thereby optimal results) of governance in geographically decoupled cyberspace may lead to a whole new set of conceptions regarding online citizenship.

Current "real-world" concepts of citizenship may not fit well within a world whose "citizens"—known only by login IDs or e-mail addresses—may concurrently participate in many online polities. Fortunately, the very ease with which users can choose to exit an online space (in notable contrast to the high cost of leaving a geographically defined politically sovereign territory) provides an alternative mechanism for preserving a "voice" for "netizens" in the context of Internet self-governance. In essence, users will be directly subjected to the rules established by sysops only for those online places that they choose to visit and revisit. If users don't find local rules for an online space congenial, they can leave that space and, indeed—cheaply enough—create their own. They can also embed their time and attention in multiple online spaces, thereby finding just that mix of rule sets that best suits their needs.

Rules on the Internet will thus be subjected to popular will by means of "voting with one's modem" rather than by means of traditional balloting or the election of representatives. In the online context, the check against sysop tyranny is not "one person, one vote" but, rather, ease of exit. And there is reason to believe that the combination of decentralized rule-making by means of (1) the unilateral actions of sysops to define online spaces, and (2) the unilateral decisions by users to join or leave such spaces, will arrive at a good solution to the collective-action problem. This is because the establishment of rules for online spaces by those who participate in those spaces will *both* (1) provide the "federalism" benefits of the "patching" algorithm, and (2) insofar as most effects of action in online fora are predominantly felt "locally" within those fora, reconnect the "congruence" between spillover sets and political decision-making bodies.

Additional good reasons exist for believing that this decentralized solution to the Net governance problem will prove optimal: Individuals are in a better position than territorially elected representatives to know how actions taken within particular online venues affect their own personal utility. Therefore, if we reduce the governance role of territorial sovereigns, those individuals who are most intensely affected by, and who care most about, the effects of online actions can be relied upon to influence optimally the relevant decision-making processes.[25] Using their newly granted ability to "enter" and "exit" political venues at will, the individuals most directly affected will have the most say in choosing the rules applicable to actions that cause such effects.

What emerges from this analysis is little short of a new definition of "civic virtue" in the online context. Based on the lessons from complex systems suggesting that multiple and competing rule sets may pull and tug each other down ridges and up higher hills in policy fitness space, we may not need to ask online citizens to adopt a frame of mind that sets aside personal or "local" interests in order to deliberate, directly or via representatives, regarding some globally applicable laws. Nor will we judge the effectiveness of Internet governance by its ability to foster rational and thoughtful deliberation among elected delegates who seek to define and serve some overall "public good." Rather, Internet governance can be judged on a systems design level by whether, and to what degree, it has adopted algorithms that effectively and substantially (but not totally) couple spillover effects with political decision-making, thus preserving congruence, and optimal legitimacy and internalization, while still allowing an adequate pull and tug among contending "local" constituencies.

Internet governance should be so constituted that the overall matrix of individuals with conflicting goals makes steady progress towards a higher and higher aggregate level of utility (that is, succeeds in its collective pursuit of happiness). Individuals will participate in this decentralized, complex, emergent form of law-making by taking many different roles as participants in many different online spaces with different rules. Our "collective conversation" about what sets of rules to adopt will continue in this new context, but it may now take the form of a complex interaction among discrete online spaces rather than that of a rational debate among a small group of elected representatives authorized to impose uniform rules from on high.

This new form of governance will also play havoc with our notions of the virtues of equality. Rather than judging Internet governance with reference to the well-being of a conceptualized standard "citizen" whose vote is entitled to equal weight in selecting representatives who then act on behalf of the populace as a whole, each Internet user will, directly, have differing degrees of influence in setting, encouraging, abiding by, and escaping from differing sets of rules for differing online spaces—depending on where each individual decides to embed time and attention in the online world. This direct involvement by "netizens" in establishing the rules that govern online life will not have the principal vice of "direct democracy"—because no tyrannical or selfish majority will be able to impose its will on an unwilling minority. (Those opposing the rules of a particular space will simply leave that virtual town and filter out disagreeable packets coming from that location.) Nor will rules established by such decentralized means be unenforceable. (It will be relatively easy for the cybersheriff of a given online town to banish wrongdoers.) Nor will rules necessarily be "unfairly" or arbitrarily applied. (Users can demand, by their usual means of threatening desertion, any particular degree of "due process" they may find desirable for particular online venues.)

Nevertheless, this new form of governance will require us to rethink what it means to be a good "citizen" in the online context—and what degree of "equal protection" is or is not assured by such status. The collective-action problem—the problem of finding an optimal solution to the complex and conflicting needs and desires of individuals—cannot be solved fully without paying attention to the impact on such individuals of the very actions they take in addressing these problems. Those who see themselves as citizens of a geographically defined sovereignty derive some of their own conceptions of well-being from that vision. The ability of the Internet to introduce positive and negative effects across those geographic borders can thus be seen either as a threat or as an opportunity to *redefine* the geographical or political group that defines what is permitted to us. Those online users who reconceptualize themselves as participating in groups that could become substantially, collectively *self-governing* without regard to geographic boundaries (using desertion, banishment, and software-code boundaries to limit unwanted actions and spillovers), will begin to reconceptualize themselves in terms of their multiple contingent participations in such groups. In that context, the highest form of "civic virtue" for the Internet may become not dispassionate concern for a uniformly defined public good but, rather, the grant and enjoyment of a freedom to travel—virtually—among online groups without restriction. And, from that perspective, the highest goal of geographically based governments concerned with the well-being of their own local citizens may become provision of the tools (including both access and education) necessary to facilitate such empowered freedom of movement.

Perhaps the most troubling aspect of any suggestion that we turn to a new form of civic virtue for governance of the Net is that none of the characteristics of this new mode of collective action appears necessarily to respect the liberty and unique value of individual elements. We're not sure, on first reflection, that we want to be treated as if we were light bulbs! Is the method we propose for finding the highest "fitness" level for the overall matrix flawed by the standard vices of utilitarianism: the lack of protection for individuals? What is to prevent the group, in its search for the highest peak on the policy fitness landscape, from throwing the interests of a contrarian individual off the nearest cliff?

We think the answer to this important question is that a diverse set of rule spaces, coupled with real freedom of movement, structurally respects individual liberty (and minority opinions about values) to the greatest extent possible, even as compared with democratic top-down rule. Unlike a standard utilitarian calculus, the patching algorithm does not try to find and impose a single answer, based on weighting each vote equally and then allowing the majority to rule. Instead, it allows all individuals selectively and partially to embed (and create) their own identities in any mix of online rule spaces and activities they find most empowering. The patching algorithm may enable particular online spaces to expel dissenters, but it also enables minorities to create their own more congenial online homes. If optimal congruence is preserved, the architecture of patching keeps the members of the overall online community sufficiently engaged with one another that they must continuously participate in a new form of online "conversation" with those who do not share their values. Even in those cases in which particular value systems are so at odds that total banishment or filtering removes some online spaces from any social intercourse with one another, those decisions must be made deliberately—and can now be made by all individuals as well as powerful officials speaking for sovereigns. In short, the complex world of diverse, decentralized, "federalist" rule-making for the Net will not perfectly preserve equality, nor respect every individual's views in every context, but it may well best serve liberty and personal empowerment interests just as it serves the goal of finding rules that best satisfy the needs of groups to seek their collective vision of the highest public good.

What we think we have shown—and that cyberspace is showing us every day—is that geographically based sovereignty, even as exercised by representative democracies, will not best solve collective-action problems in cyberspace. We think it's also clear there are serious reasons to worry about any push towards global "harmonization" that loses the clearly beneficial effects of diversity, experimentation, and local self-determination—the ability of a "patching" algorithm to force the overall system downhill, off a local optimum, towards higher ground. Instead, we think that those concerned with the governance of cyberspace may find it better to rely on decentralized decision-making by the groups most directly affected by their own online activities, leaving it up to the unpredictable pull and tug between contending rule sets to find the combination of policies that is optimal in aggregate.

CONCLUSION

Americans have been fond of saying that representative democracy is the worst form of government except for all the other alternatives. In the special context of a need to govern the online world, however, there may indeed be a better alternative. Participants in online spaces cannot readily make use of the basic ideas of geographically defined representative democracy. There is no way to meaningfully provide equal votes to online "citizens," who are not for this purpose whole people entirely located in particular territorially defined "places." Law-making for diverse online spaces should not be centralized in any single global government, even a democratic one, much less one created by the slow, incomplete, and undemocratic treaty process. Legitimacy cannot be preserved by allowing existing geographical sovereigns to assert inconsistent and asymmetrical control over all online activities that might have any impact on their citizens. But the task of setting rules for online spaces can be cut into workable pieces. And the collective-action and liberty problems can be solved simultaneously for online spaces by relying on the decisions of participants to join (or leave) those areas with rules they find empowering (or oppressive).

The new science of complex systems gives reason to hope that an overall system of Internet governance that reconnects rule-making for online spaces with those most affected by those rules—and that also allows online groups to make decentralized decisions that have some impact on others, and that therefore elicit disparate responsive strategies—will create a new form of civic virtue. The old hope that rational debate among wise elected representatives will result in the overall public good may be replaced, online at least, by a new certainty that dispersed and complex interactions among groups of individuals taking unilateral actions to serve "local" goals will be best for everyone, overall, over time.

ENDNOTES

The authors thank Jeff Williams for his superb assistance in developing and implementing the computer-based complex systems discussed herein. Thanks also to Larry Lessig, Dawn Nunziato, Mark Lemley, Warren Schwartz, David Skeel, Peter Swire, Steve Salop, and Avery Katz for both their assistance in formulating many of the ideas expressed herein and their comments on earlier drafts. Helpful comments were also provided by Jack Goldsmith, Peter Menell, and other participants at the Olin Law and Economics Symposium on International Economic Regulation at Georgetown University Law Center, 5 April 1997, and participants at the Aspen Institute's "Internet as Platform" conference at Wye River, 19–20 June 1997. We also gratefully acknowledge our obvious debt to the work of Stuart Kauffman. We welcome comments; you may e-mail us at david.johnson@counsel.com and postd@erols.com.

1. David R. Johnson and David G. Post, *Law and Borders: The Rise of Law in Cyberspace,* 48 Stanford L Rev, 1367 (1996), available online at http://www.cli.org/X0025_LBFIN.html.
2. See Jeffrey Abramson's contribution to this volume for a discussion of citizenship and community on the Internet.
3. Consider, for example, a set of rules regarding copyright in creative expression. If sovereign X adopts a strong property rule, that may inure to the benefit of authors from other jurisdictions (at least to the extent that their work is subject to protection in X). Conversely, a weak rule may produce negative externalities, diminishing the welfare of individuals in those other jurisdictions.
4. We recognize that sovereigns do also on occasion govern actions that occur outside their territories insofar as such actions are held to have an impact on the sovereigns' citizens. That special case does not, however, detract from the general rule that sovereigns control those they can readily reach by means of physical force.
5. See, for example, James Madison's discussion of optimal "extent of territory" in *The Federalist Papers,* number 10.
6. Note that we are not asserting that activities in cyberspace do not have offline effects; our claim, rather, is that whatever those effects may be, they are most often distributed more-or-less randomly with respect to geographical location.
7. See Dan Burk, *Federalism in Cyberspace,* 28 Conn L Rev, 1095 (1996). Because the Internet Protocol calls for "geographically extended sharing of scattered resources," Burk writes, users

> may therefore be completely unaware where the resource being accessed is, in fact, physically located. So insensitive is the network to geography, that it is frequently impossible to determine the physical location of a resource or user [because] such information is unimportant to the network's function [and] the network's design thus makes little provision for geographic discernment. (1098–99)

See also Joel Reidenberg, "Governing Networks and Rule-Making in Cyberspace," in *Borders in Cyberspace*, ed. Brian Kahin and Charles Nesson (Cambridge: MIT Press, 1996), 84, 85–87, which describes the destruction of territorial and substantive borders in cyberspace.

The system of machine addressing on the Internet is discussed in Dan Burk, *Trademarks Along the Infobahn: A First Look at the Emerging Law of Cybermarks,* Richmond J L & Tech (1995), available online only, at http://www.urich.edu/~jolt/v1i1/burk.html; Robert Shaw, *Internet Domain Names: Whose Domain is This?* available online only, at http://www.itu.int/intreg/dns.html; Jon Postel, *Domain Name System Structure and Delegation,* RFC 1591 (March 1994), available online only, at http://www.internic.net/rfc/rfc1591.txt.

8. It is, we note, not entirely clear how such a network redesign could achieve a congruence between machine addressing and physical location sufficient to identify a communicating machine's physical location from its address alone. There are, of course, optional country-specific location designators in use under the current Internet domain-naming conventions (e.g., "www.abc.fr," "www.xyz.jp"), where top-level domains (*.fr and *.jp, in this example) have a geographic referent (France and Japan, respectively). But currently, there are no countries that require, as a matter of domestic law, that machines within their geographic boundaries use such a country designator; no registries that can prevent individuals holding such a country designator from assigning that designator to machines in other countries; and no means to limit the use of technical protocols such as Telnet that allow users to access the Internet from other Internet access points (with other addresses). Nor, perhaps most importantly, is the use of non–country-specific designators (e.g., *.com, *.org, and so on) restricted in any geographical way.

    And we note further that the link between physical location and machine addressing appears to be substantially diminishing in recent years; the use of non-localizable global domains (e.g., *.org, *.com) is increasingly supplanting Internet domain names that include country designators such as *.fr and *.jp. See, e.g., R. Bush, B. Carpenter, and J. Postel, "Delegation of International Top Level Domains (iTLDs)" (January 1996), available at http://www/internic.net/internet-drafts/draft-ymbk-itld-admin-00.txt; and Jon Postel, "New Registries and the Delegation of International Top Level Domains," available online at http://www/internic.net/internet-drafts/draft-postel-iana-itld-admin-00.txt.

    A recent proposal by the Internet Ad Hoc Coalition, a group including the Internet Society and the Internet Engineering Task Force, has proposed modifying the domain name system to, inter alia, increase the potential number of global non-localizable domain names. See "Final Report of the International Ad Hoc Committee: Recommendations for Administration and Management of gTLDs," available online at http://www.iahc.org.

9. Johnson and Post, *Law and Borders,* 1375 and 1375, n. 23. For a wealth of information about the architecture of the Usenet network, see "What is Usenet?" available online at http://www.smartpages.com/bngfaqs/news/announce/newusers/top.html, and http://www.cam.org/~intsci/newsmail.html.

10. Suppose, for example, that the two jurisdictions have importantly differing rules about what constitutes permissible (not actionably infringing) "fair use."

11. Our findings are presented in more detail in our paper "Borders, Spillovers, and Complexity: Rule-Making Processes in Cyberspace (and Elsewhere)," presented at the Olin Law and Economics Symposium on International Economic

Regulation at Georgetown University Law Center, Washington, D.C., April 1997. Copies of the paper are available from the authors.

12. The best introductions to Stuart Kauffman's work can be found in his *The Origins of Order: Self Organization and Selection in Evolution* (New York: Oxford University Press, 1993) and *At Home in the Universe* (New York: Oxford University Press, 1995).

13. We recognize that arguments based on the aggregate results of the patching algorithm will, in increasing overall utility, raise concerns about distributional equity and liberty. As more fully discussed near the end of this chapter, we think those concerns are best answered by recognition that, in the context of diverse online rule sets, individuals are free to embed their time and attention in multiple "patches"—and can thus choose the mix of online rules that they find most empowering. While both education and differences in access and real-world economics will constrain any effort to achieve "equality" among individuals, there is no reason, in the context of such governance mechanisms for the online world, to think that we should *not* be striving to increase the "utility" of the aggregate and of the average individual participant.

14. Or, shifting the level of granularity, each element might be an individual country, the state of whose copyright laws may affect "utility"—the condition of authors, publishers, and consumers of information—in numerous other jurisdictions.

15. See discussion at the end of this chapter regarding the distributional and liberty effects of the alternative governance system we propose.

16. Because of the obvious significance of intellectual property laws in this new medium, the single patch/global harmonization strategy for cyberspace has perhaps been most forcefully pressed in this context. See National Information Infrastructure Task Force, "Intellectual Property and the National Information Infrastructure" (Washington, D.C.: Government Printing Office, 1994), 132, for a statement of Clinton administration positions in favor of "efforts to work toward a new level of international harmonization" of international copyright law. See also Raymond Nimmer, *Licensing on the Global Information Infrastructure: Disharmony in Cyberspace*, 16 J Intl L Bus, 224, 246–47 (1995). As Nimmer notes about the Global Information Infrastructure (GII):

> The multinational character of GII-related property and contract law creates potentially huge problems for the development of commercial relationships relating to information and other intangible property moved through and around the GII. *More so here than in any prior commercial/economic context, an enhanced degree of harmonization and simplification is needed* to enable the transactions made possible by the technology to occur. (246–47; emphasis added)

See Charles Goldring, "Netting the Cybershark: Consumer Protection, Cyberspace, the Nation-State, and Democracy," in Kahin and Nesson, eds., *Borders in Cyberspace*, 322, 340–44, which argues that because cyberspace activities know no national boundaries, harmonization of intellectual property laws is necessary. See also Charles McManis, *Taking Trips on the Information Superhighway: International Intellectual Property Protection and Emerging*

Computer Technology, 41 Vill L Rev, 207 (1995), which discusses efforts to harmonize international trademark and unfair competition laws. The recently concluded meetings called by the World Intellectual Property Organization to consider proposals to modify the Berne Convention for Literary and Artistic Property is a prime example of an attempt to implement this strategy.

In regard to other legal regimes, see Joseph Grundfest, *Internationalization of the World's Securities Markets: Economic Causes and Regulatory Consequences*, 4 J Fin Svcs Res, 349 (1990), which discusses the drive to increase global harmonization of securities laws in response to the increasing frequency of cross-border transactions); and Louis Solomon and Louise Corso, *The Impact of Technology on the Trading of Securities: The Emerging Global Market and the Implications for Regulation*, 24 John Marshall L Rev, 299, 330 (1991), which notes the difficult choice of legal problems posed by cyberspace securities markets, and suggests that "adoption of a uniform international law by all nations would surely be an ideal solution to the problems of internationalization." See also Michael Rustad and Lori Eisenschmidt, *The Commercial Law of Internet Security*, 10 High Tech L J, 213, 300 (1995), which notes the demand among commentators for a "uniform commercial law of the Internet."

17. U.S. export administration act regulations, which declare encryption technology to constitute a "munitions" technology subject to licensing by the Department of Commerce prior to export, are discussed in National Research Council, "Cryptography's Role in Securing the Information Society" (June 1996), available online at http://pwp.usa.pipeline.com/~jya/nrcindex.htm. Also see, generally, A. Michael Froomkin, *The Metaphor is the Key: Cryptography, the Clipper Chip, and the Constitution*, 143 U Pa L Rev, 709 (1995).

18. See Johnson and Post, *Law and Borders*, which describes German attempts to suppress Usenet activity. See also Karen Kaplan, "Germany Forces Online Service to Censor Internet," *Los Angeles Times*, 29 December 1995, A1; and Ruth Walker, "Why Free-Wheeling Internet Hit Teutonic Wall over Porn," *Christian Science Monitor*, 4 January 1996, 1. Kara Swisher's "Cyberporn Debate Goes International; Germany Pulls the Shade on CompuServe, Internet," *Washington Post*, 1 January 1996, F13, describes efforts by a local Bavarian police force that had the effect of requiring CompuServe to temporarily cut off the availability of news groups to its entire audience (at least until a way to prevent delivery of specified groups to the German audience could be developed). Although CompuServe was initially compliant, it subsequently rescinded the ban on most of the files, sending parents a new program to choose for themselves what items to restrict. Also see "CompuServe Ends Access Suspension: It Reopens All But Five Adult-Oriented Newsgroups. Parents Can Now Block Offensive Material," *Los Angeles Times*, 14 February 1996, D1.

19. See Johnson and Post, *Law and Borders*. See also A. Michael Froomkin, "The Internet as a Source of Regulatory Arbitrage," in Kahin and Nesson, eds., *Borders in Cyberspace*, 140–42, which describes the difficulties inherent in any attempt by the government of "Ruritania" to prevent communication between its citizens and those in other countries.

20. The Minnesota Attorney General's Office distributed a "Warning to All Internet Users and Providers" (available at http://www.state.mn.us/cbranch/ag/memo/txt), which stated that "Persons outside of Minnesota who transmit information via the Internet knowing that information will be disseminated in Minnesota are subject to jurisdiction in Minnesota courts for violations of state criminal and civil laws" (emphasis omitted). The conclusion rested on the Minnesota general criminal jurisdiction statute, which provides that "a person may be convicted and sentenced under the law of this State if the person . . . (3) Being without the state, intentionally causes a result within the state prohibited by the criminal laws of this State." Minn Stat Ann § 609.025 (West 1987). Minnesota also began civil proceedings against Wagernet, a Nevada gambling business that posted an Internet advertisement for online gambling services. See *Complaint, Minnesota v Granite Gate Resorts, Inc.* (1995; No. 9507227), available online at http://www.state.mn.us/ebranch/ag/ggcom.txt. A Minnesota trial court judge recently upheld personal jurisdiction over the defendant in Minnesota. See *State of Minnesota v Granite Gate Resorts, Inc.,* available online at http://www.ag.state.mn.us/consumer/news/OnlineScams/; http://www.leepfrog.com/E-Law/Cases/Minn_v_Granite_Gate.html. Also see, generally, Mark Eckenwiler, "States Get Entangled in the Web," *Legal Times,* 22 January 1996, S35.

21. See Dan Burk, "The Market for Digital Piracy," in Kahin and Nesson, eds., *Borders in Cyberspace,* 220–221, which describes the "race to externalize" given the spillover effects of the Internet on the market for intellectual property law products; see also Burk, *Federalism in Cyberspace,* 28 U Conn L Rev, 1095 (1996). As Roberta Romano's *The Genius of American Corporate Law* (Washington, D.C.: American Enterprise Press, 1993), notes:

> A state will not want to pay for benefits experienced by nonresidents, for example [and may wish to] export the cost of providing goods and services for [its] residents to nonresidents, for instance by adopting taxes that are more likely to be paid by out-of-state than in-state individuals or firms. (5)

> See also Clark Gillette, *In Partial Praise of Dillon's Rule, or, Can Public Choice Theory Justify Local Government Law?* 67 Chi-Kent L Rev, 959 (1991), which argues that outside the idealized world of no inter-jurisdictional externalities, some constraints on local power are justified "to prevent strategic local behavior"; Frank Easterbrook and Daniel Fischel, *Mandatory Disclosure and the Protection of Investors,* 70 Va L Rev, 669 (1984), which observes that the multistate nature of securities markets creates strategic opportunities for states to attempt to exploit investors who live elsewhere.

22. Lawrence Lessig has written insightfully about the ways in which software code effectively enforces the virtual boundaries between online spaces. See Lessig, *Constitution and Code,* 27 Cumb L Rev, 1 (1997).

23. A recent decision by some collaborating sysops to send "cancel" messages for all UUNet traffic directed towards Usenet newsgroups, and by many sysops receiving these messages to implement them, represents just this sort of collective-action fil-

tering. The "Usenet Death Penalty" is controversial, because it is aimed at an entire group of users, only a few of whom are originating "wrongful" messages. Its proponents argue that they have no alternative other than to act against the Internet Service Provider (UUNet) that "harbors" this form of wrongdoing. The technical and social pull and tug among spammers and their enemies can be expected to continue.

24. See Madison, *The Federalist Papers*, number 10.

25. Not only are individuals more likely to be in possession of the relevant information regarding the effect of cross-border and inter-jurisdictional spillover on their own lives, they can also act more quickly on that information than can agents at a higher level of the organizational hierarchy (i.e., their elected representatives) to whom that information must be redirected and through whom it must be reprocessed before "official" boundary realignment can occur. In other words, putting boundary definition in the hands of individuals allows a faster and more flexible response to rapidly changing spillover patterns. See Friedrich Hayek, "Notes on the Evolution of Systems of Rules of Conduct," in his *Studies in Philosophy, Politics, and Economics* (Chicago: University of Chicago Press, 1967), 66–81, which suggests that a single-stage, polycentric order without a "directing center" need not be inferior to a "hierarchic order" because it dispenses with the necessity of communicating to a common center all the information on which its several elements act.

THE INTERNET
AND COMMUNITY

Jeffrey Abramson

Louis Stulberg Professor of Law and Politics
Brandeis University

According to a 1997 Lou Harris/Baruch College poll, 57 percent of Americans who use the Internet repeatedly access the same sites.[1] This finding suggests that the now-familiar metaphors comparing Internet users to "surfers" or "nomads" wandering randomly from one site to the next may no longer provide accurate images of online behavior. As Paul Curtis put it in a 1994 *CPSR Newsletter*, the Internet is "not a highway but a place."[2] Reminiscent of connections made at coffee houses, bars, or (in former pen-pal days) through the mail, accessing the Internet today is for many persons a way to find people as well as information— and to overcome the ways in which time and geography have heretofore limited conversation.

Other data confirm the shift on the World Wide Web from "surfers" to "homesteaders," "community-builders," and "netizens." Visits to many Web sites increase by as much as 50 percent when the capacity to "chat" is added to the site.[3] Moreover, according to a University of Minnesota study, chat visitors stay at a given site for an average of 30 minutes, as opposed to the 7-minute average visit to non-chat sites.[4] America Online (AOL) claims to support 14,000 different chat rooms, accounting for one-third of members' time online. In addition, AOL's popular "instant message" feature allows any two persons to create their own two-person chat room by exchanging instant e-mail messages in real time with text scrolling up on the screen as it is sent and received.

(In 1997, AOL sold this "instant message" technology to Netscape, thus enlarging the arena of instant messaging.) "Buddy lists" alert members as to which of their friends are currently online so that they can exchange these instant messages. All of which leads AOL Studios president Theodore Leonsis to say that "community is the Velcro that keeps people there."[5]

In 1994, when there were still only about a million Americans on the Internet, most of whom were young, computer-savvy, and self-described explorers, the surfer metaphor was clearly more apt than it was by 1997, when an estimated 40 million Americans had Internet access,[6] many of whom had far less computer know-how than "surfers" and, consequently, a far greater need to gravitate to sites they could call home. The 1997 Lou Harris/Baruch College poll found that two-thirds of U.S. Internet users were now 30 years old or older, including 19 percent over the age of 50.[7] To much of this new population, the Internet at first "feels like jumping out into the ocean," remarks Douglas Rushkoff, author of *Cyberbia*. "Online communities provide the lifeguards."[8] Moreover, because the worldwide population with access to the Internet is expected to jump from an estimated 25 million users in 1995 to 217 million by the year 2000,[9] the American-style shift from "surfers" to "homesteaders" is likely to be duplicated abroad.

Another startling change in Internet usage is the rapid closing of the online gender gap. As recently as 1995, women accounted for only 23 percent of all U.S. Internet users. That percentage has now risen to 41 percent.[10] Although no survey has definitively shown that women gravitate to different kinds of Web sites than do men, the question of gender differences is clearly relevant to the kind of conversations and connections the Internet will evolve to support.

On a superficial level, it is clear that most online communities are united by common interest in a particular subject-matter, be it plants, tips on raising children, chat aimed at twentysomethings, women's issues, or farm news.[11] However, many astute commentators about online communities insist that the *content* of conversation on a particular site is not the crucial attraction that brings people back repeatedly.[12] To be sure, it's content that first brings golfers to GolfWeb and New Age intellectuals to Utne Online.[13] But, says Tom Rielly, CEO of the online gay community PlanetOut, "it's not the content. It's the people, stupid. Content may be why people visit a site. But community is why people stay."[14] Sony Online Vice President Matt Rothman agrees: "In the chat rooms," he says, "people essentially become the content."[15] This is especially true of discussion groups such as are often found on Usenet, the Internet bulletin board system, where discussion takes place without a moderator.

But exactly what *are* online or virtual communities? Does chat alone a community make? Chat about any subject at all for any amount of time with any number of different persons? Even chat in Usenet discussion groups with subject headings such as "alt.sex.beastiality" or "alt.sex.bondage"? Perhaps an even more primary question is in order: Assuming people know an Internet community when they see one, why should they want to join it in the first place? Don't people already have enough community contact in real space, in schools and churches, through voluntary activities, political parties, and so on?

Whole volumes have already been penned, addressing these slippery questions and trumpeting the Internet's potential to virtually reinvent the nature of human association after the millennium.[16] But for all the fanfare about virtual communities, little sober analysis has sought to discover what is lacking in real communities and how online communities can grow from casual chat into stable, intimate associations worthy of the name "community." Even arriving at a common definition of community is notoriously difficult; what seems vital to one person may be supernumerary or even irrelevant to another. Disagreement also abounds over whether "community" (whatever it is) is on the rise or decline in various nations, as well as over which communities are the good ones, and which the bad ones.

In this chapter, I will discuss the political theory of community and the use of the Internet by community-oriented people for the purposes both of reviving local community and building virtual community. I begin with an attempt to clarify the meaning and value of this mysterious term "community."

WHAT IS "COMMUNITY"?

"Community" is a notoriously ambiguous word. Cities and towns and all manner of physical places are customarily called communities merely because they constitute a contiguous geographical space. When geography alone qualifies an enclosed population as a community, even the bedroom suburb earns the honorific title. So, too, geography explains talk of national communities, though in most nation-states the centrifugal forces of ethnicity or language-based cultures belie the myth of *e pluribus unum* ("out of many, one").

Sometimes people refer to communities based on "interests," in which members understand their membership primarily in instrumental terms. (How can this group help me achieve my own goals in life?) Professors scattered across the land form the academic community; lawyers, the legal community; artists and their patrons, the art world. A lover of Puccini opera may find she has more in common with physically remote opera buffs than with her own geographical neighbors.

"Intimacy," rather than special interests, defines other communities. Whereas sharing interests makes only for an interest group, sharing intimacy turns a group into an emotionally involved association.

Finally, there are religious communities, ethnic communities, spiritual communities, and the like. For these communities, devotion to one's religion or people is frequently an end in itself, part of what it means to become "the person I am." (When this sort of allegiance becomes total, irrational, and destructive, it earns the name "cult.")

These differing concepts of community sometimes coexist comfortably. John Smith might well be a practicing Catholic professor of logic who has just moved to Bethesda, Maryland, and travels to the Kennedy Center in Washington, D.C., whenever Puccini is on the bill. He belongs to several communities simultaneously and without contradiction. But clashes are possible. Bethesda may be prejudiced against an influx of Catholics; Puccini lovers may be snobs when it comes to town support for their John-Philip-Sousa–loving neighbors who march in the American Legion band. These tensions illustrate ways in which geographical communities (especially of the bedroom-suburb sort) may not be a foundation for the common good at all. They also illustrate how geographical communities can become factionalized and balkanized into the more particular subcommunities within their borders. In democracies from ancient Rome to today's United States, a paramount question of politics has been how to honor communal differences while moving toward a more universal, national allegiance.

Despite these ambiguities, rigorous use of the word "community" refers to an association defined by the following characteristics:

- *Shared purpose or common good.* A group is a community only when its members understand themselves to be participants in a common way of life. Some groups lack this characteristic because they really are no more than instruments through which members pursue their private or personal interests. In a genuine community, political theorist Michael Sandel notes, individuals unite to defend a good in common that no one of them could achieve alone.[17]

- *Equality.* Ideally, a community treats all of its members as equally worthy of respect. Thus, there is no genuinely common way of life possible when a group of men rules over women, or where public discrimination judges a person on the basis of race, religion, gender, national origin, age, or handicap. Of course, actual groups regularly fall short of the ideal of perfect equality and yet manage to inspire enough confidence in members to qualify as genuine communities; the fact that humans are bound to fall short of realizing our ideals does not alter the moral status of those ideals.

- *Loyalty.* Communities inspire solidarity, allegiance, and patriotism. At a minimum, members must experience something akin to intimacy with their fellow members. The intimacy need not be as intense as family ties or as passionate as love, but it must move people to experience their membership in the community as vital to their own personal identities. Roughly speaking, members of a community must feel the bonds of citizenship. Thus, for example, members of Phi Beta Kappa do not constitute a community because their "fraternity" is wholly external to their sense of self. Contrast this to the situation of a religiously observant person for whom "being part of the congregation" is internal to her own identity.

- *Autonomy/Self-government.* Communities must have the power and autonomy to create and practice their own ways of life. Without such power, groups' meetings and conversations are idle; everyone knows beforehand that nothing of consequence flows from their chat, that power resides elsewhere and above. Under such conditions, citizens lose interest in assembling and approach talk as "cheap."

- *Space.* Traditionally, communities occupy physical or geographical space. Members meet, assemble, congregate in town halls, town meetings, religious congregations, choruses, parks, street corner societies, coffee houses, bars, theaters, clubs, and halls. Even communities of interest hold annual meetings of the American Bar Association, the American Medical Association, and so on. The importance of space to community is not just symbolic. Rather, face-to-face meetings *create* community by engaging individuals in deliberation about the purposes and the plans of a community.

- *Deliberation.* Deliberative communication is the essence of community; give-and-take debate habituates people to reconsider their own interests and opinions in light of what is good for the whole. A community without meetings is a group without citizens.

- *Numbers.* Physical community is inversely proportional to population size and geographical area: The more people and/or the greater the territory, the weaker are the ties that bind persons together. At some point, a group becomes too large to form a community or else the miles separating its members are too great to bridge. While no mathematical formula tells us when the obstacles of size and territory become insurmountable, people intuitively understand the finite limits to community.

These factors, then—shared purpose, the ideal of equality, loyalty, autonomy, shared space, deliberation, and appropriate size—define associations that can, with rigor, be called communities.

THE POLITICAL THEORY OF COMMUNITY

Intellectual interest in community-building through the Internet is generally part of a broader critique that begins by stressing the vital connection between tight community and strong democracy.[18] Dating back to the French philosopher Alexis de Tocqueville's praise of the abundance of voluntary associations in America, the critique argues that democracy rises or falls on its ability to instill in citizens a sense of shared purpose, and that only active involvement in civic affairs yokes individuals to the common good. In short, without community there is no moral compass to guide individuals from individual self-government (the opportunity to assert self-interest) to communal self-government (participation in, and responsibility for, the public good).

Consider, in light of this critique, the status of community in the United States today. Alarmingly, the cohesiveness of community—especially local community—is in decline if measured by the power of voluntary associations to forge a common identity among inhabitants of the same physical space. Churches, schools, public libraries, fraternal orders, parent-teacher organizations, charitable groups, labor unions, main streets, parades, and patriotic holidays seem all to be losing their hold on the public imagination. This condition is in stark contrast to an earlier age described by Theodore White, author of the *Making of the President* books. White tells how he found his own sense of national citizenship—against all odds of poverty and discrimination—inside the bowels of the Boston Public Library. There he could escape from the parochialism of life in an ethnic neighborhood into a larger, common culture of learning.[19] Generations of immigrants could tell similar stories of the importance of some school or library to their entrance into a larger community.

Although the traditional watering-holes for community still survive, they often seem overmatched by globalizing forces that dwarf the resources of local institutions. The local town meeting or city council is usually powerless to control the decisions of a Staples or a Sears to open or close a store. The jurisdiction of a town's Natural Resources Commission stops at the town's borders but the sources of pollution do not. At the same time, public space for community is being undermined from below by the VCR/cable/computer/home-entertainment revolution that keeps citizens amused and informed at home in isolation from each other. Given these realities of life in the global-economy-*cum*-home-theater, is it any wonder that citizens do not flock to the town meeting or commission hearing?

The current picture is not entirely bleak, however: In 1996 the Roper Organization released data showing that, since 1990, civic participation in some arenas (for example, environmental campaigns) is on the rise.[20] Indeed, community organizing among issues-oriented groups such as gay or disabled Americans is only now coming into its own. Even so, the politics of identity practiced by many so-called "hyphenated" Americans potentially balkanizes the larger community into ethnic enclaves or one-issue constituencies. Yet so has it ever been: Those who praise traditional community oversell its moral worth when they overlook the fact that the very intimacy that makes a group into a community can degenerate into parochial prejudice and narrow-minded sameness.

The best of those who advocate the reinvigoration of community are the most unromantic students of community's past, the so-called "New Communitarians."[21] Acknowledging the dark side of community closeness, the New Communitarians nonetheless see the strengthening of democracy as depending on massive investment in "social capital," to use the term of political scientist Robert Putnam.[22] "Social capital" refers to the myriad of ways in which joining the parent-teacher organization, singing in the church choir, and even bowling in a league bring people together around a shared purpose, a joint enterprise, a common good.

THE INTERNET AS A PLATFORM FOR COMMUNITY

Let us now return to the particular forms that "community" takes on the Internet. Even a cursory tour of the Internet shows that all kinds of meetings, forums, and conferences are taking place in cyberspace. Consider, for instance, the phenomenon of e-mail, one that has virtually revived the habit of letter-writing. The 1997 Harris/Baruch College poll found that 89 percent of all U.S. Internet users make use of e-mail; one-third of these consider themselves to belong to some online community by virtue of their e-mail exchanges.[23]

Chat rooms make intimates of people with a shared passion for *Star Wars* (the movie). "Listservs" sustain a collaborative conversation about slavery among historians.[24] The "Jury Rights Project" puts together and mobilizes a political coalition to protest a Colorado judge's decision to hold juror Laura Kriho in contempt of court for an act of jury nullification.[25] In 1995, students in Wellesley, Massachusetts, and Des Moines, Iowa, studied about, and then talked online to Rosa Parks. After Parks departed, the students paired off with electronic partners to discuss civil rights and race relations in their respective communities. "UptoDate" carries potentially life-saving online exchanges among doctors about the latest advances in medical procedures.[26] In a less serious vein, the

Star Trek scriptwriter-"wannabe" collective writes, edits, and publishes would-be scripts for the TV series.[27]

As Doug Schuler of the Seattle Community Network points out, two main features of computer networking support community participation.[28] First, the Internet is a "many-to-many" medium as opposed to television's "one-to-many" broadcasting. Television promotes passivity in viewers, who learn the habits of receiving messages without the resources to respond. By contrast, the Internet is a fully interactive medium that supports all kinds of criss-crossing horizontal and vertical conversations. Second, the Internet potentially democratizes information by permitting ordinary citizens to bypass gatekeepers and to access vast stores of information for themselves.[29]

Yet, all of the traditional tensions and ambiguities about community are in play when it comes to the new fabric being woven by the World Wide Web. Advocates of the Web's ability to create community generally take two differing positions. Some say the metaphor of a "global village" is the wrong one for the Internet, that localism will forever remain the sine qua non of meaningful community. These people turn to cyberspace only as a practical and efficient tool to do the traditional work of civic education and grassroots community organizing. A second group maintains that the Internet is replacing moribund geographical communities with creative virtual communities able to bring doctors or students or Trekkers together from around the world, free from the traditional constraints of too many people, too little time, and too much distance between them. These "virtual space" advocates build upon traditional communities of interest already detached from geography, only now powered by a technology that allows one to search the globe for a *Star Trek* chat in the morning, medical shop talk in the afternoon, and politics at night.

In what follows, I analyze first the Internet as a platform for traditional, local, geographic community-building. I then turn to the notion of virtual community to explore whether the Internet is revolutionizing—for better or for worse—the nature of community.

Reviving Local Community through the Internet

Some of the most exciting networks on the Internet aim to conserve rather than overthrow traditional local community. Starting with the pioneering FreeNets in Cleveland, Santa Monica, Seattle, Charlotte, and elsewhere, community activists have used computer networking as a way not only to improve delivery of basic city services (e.g., by offering electronic building permits in Cleveland) but also to restore substance to participatory democracy by sustaining deliberative conversation among ordinary citizens themselves (e.g., a discussion of how to help the homeless of Santa Monica find jobs). The Seattle Community Network's Doug Schuler claims that some 300 computer-oriented community networks now serve half a million registered users. Schuler estimates that 200 more networks were on the drawing board as of early 1997.[30]

The Cleveland FreeNet is the oldest and largest of the civic computer networks.[31] Begun in 1986, it now boasts 160,000 registered users. But scores of local communities now have their own networks, including the Mobile (Alabama) Area Free-Net, Bridgeport (Connecticut) On-Line; the Sun Coast (Tampa/St. Petersburg, Florida) Free-Net; the Panhandle (northern Idaho) Free-Net; Prairienet (east-central Illinois); BRAIN (Baton Rouge, Louisiana); Big Sky Telegraph (rural Montana); Minnesota E-Democracy; the La Plaza Telecommunity (Taos, New Mexico); Philadelphia (Pennsylvania) Neighborhoods OnLine; SENDIT (Fargo, North Dakota); and the Ozark Regional Information OnLine Net (southwest Missouri).[32]

These community-based computer networks begin with the proposition that most citizens lack the time, information, and motivation for active and informed citizenship. The networks deal with time obstacles by using the asynchronous nature of e-mail exchanges and the like; on the network, citizens on their own time schedules can ask questions of, and read answers from, city council members or fellow citizens. The networks accomplish civic education through online transcripts of town meetings and through user-friendly navigational screen maps—typically a graphical representation of a digital city on which users need only click on the icon for the appropriate building (say, the Public Health Department) to gain information (say, about mosquito spraying in their neighborhood). Finally, the networks deal with motivational problems by creating novel forums where citizens can interact with elected officials as well as with each other.

As a platform for local community, the Internet and other computer delivery systems have their benefits and drawbacks. On the positive side are civic education and equality:

Civic Education

A local citizen who wants to follow local politics can often find more information currently available via the Internet than any competing source. Take, for example, the Public Electronic Network (PEN) in Santa Monica.[33] All city organizations are online and a Santa Monica resident is promised an answer within forty-eight hours, via e-mail, to any question about city services. Moreover, busy people without time to personally attend meetings of city commissions can access online transcripts of the meetings from their home.

The Civic Practices Network (CPN) is an excellent example of civic education through the Internet.[34] Throughout the country, grassroots organizers often work in isolation from one another even though they may be tackling similar problems of crime or jobs or facing problems that spill over from and into other locales (e.g., acid rain). CPN is an online journal through which community organizers share ideas about community empowerment. According to Carmen Siriani, cofounder of CPN, the network aims to enhance the quality of local government by spreading knowledge of successful civic projects in one corner of the nation to all corners.[35] For instance, in 1997, a community organizer who clicked on the "Civic Map" on CPN's home page could access information about:

- local efforts by Safe Streets Now in Berkeley and Oakland to close down drug houses;

- use of "priority boards" in Dayton, Ohio, to bring the problems of isolated neighborhoods to the attention of city government;

- land-use planning and pollution control projects in St. Paul;

- the Nehemiah Project in East Brooklyn, which focuses on building affordable housing;

- the Dudley Street Neighborhood Initiative, and its strategies for economical revival in the Boston inner-city minority community of Roxbury.[36]

CPN also capitalizes on the linked (or webbed) nature of Internet communication to steer citizens who happen to knock on CPN's virtual door to the Web sites of similar community-support organizations. Links direct a visitor from the CPN site to 50 affiliate groups, including the Pew Center for Civic Journalism, the Center for Democracy and

Citizenship, the Morino Institute, the National Civic League, the Kettering Foundation, and others.[37] An isolated community organizer in—say—rural Tennessee can use the Internet to gain access to a whole community of community organizers sharing talk and tools about common community problems.

In an interview, Siriani noted the paradox of using "the global distributional capacity" of the Internet to support intensely local community efforts. But Siriani embraces the paradox, arguing that the Internet does not create community or even house one itself. Like other technologies, it is simply a neutral tool to support political efforts.[38]

Equality

Worldwide, the number of persons with access to the Internet is growing at a rate of 10 percent a month.[39] As previously mentioned, some estimates place the number of persons with Internet access by the year 2000 as high as 217 million.[40] While this explosive growth is made possible by declining costs, a substantial information gap between rich and poor still exists.[41] In the United States, after a slow start, communities are attempting to bridge that gap by equipping neighborhood public libraries with free computer terminals and public access to the Internet. Examples of public Internet projects include collaboration between Charlotte's Web and the Public Library of Charlotte and Mecklenburg County, North Carolina; the Cleveland Public Electronic Library; the partnership between the People for Puget Sound and the Seattle Public Library; the California State Library's Internet for People project, which provide access to the Internet through neighborhood public libraries in 180 communities; and Nebraska@Online, a partnership between the Nebraska Library Commission and community-based groups focusing on economic development.[42]

The role of the Seattle Public Library in equalizing Internet access for local residents is typical of the above projects. People for Puget Sound is a local group dedicated to preserving the Sound's ecosystem. In 1994, the group enlisted the help of the Seattle Public Library in providing Internet access about the Sound to all interested Seattle residents. The library established a Web site as well as terminals and Internet access in branch libraries. On the Web site users may click an icon for the Environmental Information Center. A further click on the "local" section provides information about upcoming events, background library material on environmental issues, and a list of volunteer opportunities. Additional links take users to related Web sites dealing with local environmental issues. A citizen who makes a connection to members of the People of Puget Sound will be directed to the U.S. Fish and Wildlife Web site to find out about endangered species in the Sound or to the Environmental Protection Agency Region 10 site to learn of local sources of dioxin poisoning and where to go to help ongoing efforts at dioxin dispersal. In short, the linked nature of Web sites allows anyone who walks into a Seattle Library with an environmental question about the Sound to explore an entire universe of information, at once broad and boundless and yet narrow and focused as the questioner wants.[43]

Another group doing yeoman's work to close the Internet access gap is the Center for Neighborhood Technology (CNT).[44] Headed by Antonia Stone and Peter Miller, CNT grew out of "Playing to Win," a pioneering effort in Harlem to bring computers and computer know-how to inner-city school children. Reasoning that local communities thrive only when local schools are good, CNT has expanded to spearhead a similar effort in the Boston area.

Attempts to equalize access to the Internet and to use it for civic education are the good news. On the negative side are six key problems with computer networks as tools for rebuilding local community:

Fragmentation

In describing the Seattle Community Network, Doug Schuler notes the open nature of the network, with space for the Lesbian Gay Bisexual Transgender Community alongside an Alcoholics Anonymous forum and postings for after-school clubs.[45] The La Plaza telecommunity in Taos is similar in hosting forums on topics ranging from art to ashrams to domestic violence to gay and lesbian sexuality.[46] Schuler is certainly right that the all-inclusiveness of these networks achieves the equality and antidiscrimination standards for genuine community. But, as he point outs, such networks can fragment rather than unite a local population, if Internet access is used to cocoon people within conversations among only their "own kind." Of course, the Internet itself does not create these factions, but the technical ease with which icons route persons to their particular subgroups might well promote it. Thus, a careful balancing act is necessary in designing community networks. Diversity in subgroup Web sites is a welcome affirmation of the heterogeneity that makes for vibrant, rich democracy. But networks also need to move those who come only to talk with like-minded people into conversations with fellow citizens who think differently.

Poor Quality of Deliberative Conversation

Conversation is the primary activity of community network users. But, as on talk radio, the conversation often rambles on or degenerates into angry tirades known in cyberspace and elsewhere as "flaming." Kent Jones, a professor of economics at Babson College, notes two factors that promote flaming on the Internet. First is anonymity. The second is the ease with which the technology allows the flamer to hit-and-run a conversation. For Jones, face-to-face conversation has a built-in dynamic that inhibits tirades; after all, you are there to see or be seen. But Internet conversation loosens inhibitions by sheltering the identity of the flamer. So, too, many chat rooms do without a moderator or an electronic equivalent of Robert's Rules of Order.[47]

Beyond issues of manners, Internet conversation is often disjointed—more a series of postings to a gigantic bulletin board than an actual conversation in real time. Listserv conversations are cases in point, as one person after another adds comments but does not really enter into the give and take of real-time conversation. Perhaps it would be more accurate to say that the give and take ultimately do occur, subject to time delays. Still, at any give moment, the intensity of the exchange is sapped by knowledge that one may be talking to an unmonitored monitor.

Privatization of Communication

The Internet is part of a continuous movement of communication from public to private space. On the one hand, home-centered communication fosters community by democratizing information and letting ordinary citizens bypass traditional gatekeepers in search of remote and sophisticated data. On the other hand, the movement of communication into private space means people no longer need to go to the library for research or assemble to talk.

The advent of the VCR led to predictions that videorecorded movies would destroy the cinema as a public medium. The opposite is happening as the habit of watching movies on video seems to be whetting the public appetite for watching the ever-latest cinematic releases.

Perhaps dire predictions about how home-centered communication over the Net is bound to destroy public libraries and other traditional public places for communication will prove equally false.

Surfing

The habit of "surfing" on the Net is unlikely to produce the slow and steady habits of talk demanded by the deliberative ideal of conversation. In deliberative conversation, people need the patience to reflect on what is said back to them, to seek out further information before responding, and to reconsider their first thoughts in light of new information. More often than not, surfers are here for one snippet, there for another, never staying through multiple iterations of discussion.

Lurking

There is nothing new or especially insidious about the fact that many Internet users sign into a discussion only to eavesdrop; these "lurkers" are akin to backbenchers in Parliament, or the silent type in face-to-face meetings. The problem is that statistics about how many people are "present" in an online forum also count the lurkers and thus exaggerate the number of active participants. Moreover, while it is easy to know who the silent ones are in a face-to-face assembly, Internet users can lurk anonymously inside chat rooms. This hardly makes for community. Nor does the fact that (at least on America Online), lurkers have less anonymity than they often assume. Once users know others' screen names, they can put them on their buddy lists, and know when they are currently signed into a chat room or forum.

Few Users

The history to date of public access channels on cable television should problematize romantic visions of techno-fixes for democracy. Local government meetings are frequently televised over public access cable channels but precious few citizens bother to tune in. Indeed the amount of persons watching a given public access channel at any particular time is so small as not to be measurable by Nielsen Service standards.[48] Similarly, political discussions on the Internet attract a band of intensely loyal followers but, as quoted above, the FreeNets throughout the country still possess only half a million subscribers among them.

Virtual Community

As previously noted, "communities of interest" with no permanent geographical base have long preexisted the Internet. But the Internet provides a powerful means for furthering the existence of these "virtual communities" by using its outreach capabilities to collect similarly interested people who, but for cyberspace, would have next to no chance of ever finding one another. Howard Rheingold's book *Virtual Community: Homesteading on the Electronic Frontier* remains the most complete survey of new virtual communities on the Net and I will not recapitulate his examples here.[49] At any rate, many virtual communities are well-known and have been around for some time now. The WELL (the Whole Earth Catalogue's Whole Earth 'Lectronic Link) dates back to 1985 in Sausalito, California, though it has been accessible through the Net rather than through telephone to a private computer only since 1995.[50] *Business Week* describes the WELL as "a salon for the digerati," supporting nearly 260 separate discussion groups at any one time.[51] Dinty Moore, author of *The Emperor's Virtual Clothes: The Naked Truth About Internet Culture*, tells the following story to illustrate the genuine bonds among WELL users: A long-time WELL regular, Elly, dropped off the system and went off to the Himalayas to become a Buddhist nun. Once there, she became ill with a dangerous liver ailment. When word of Elly's illness was posted on the WELL, regulars—including doctors and travel agents—mobilized quickly to fly her home, where she was treated and cured.[52]

In addition to the WELL, other longstanding virtual communities include ECHO (East Coast Hang Out), which started in New York City and the Spring, which started in Austin, Texas.[53] But the sophistication and cohesiveness of virtual communities have grown by leaps and bounds since the successes of these early pioneer groups and bulletin boards. Consider, for instance, a site run by the Boston-based Firefly Network, which has already registered two million users who spend an average of 32 minutes each visit.[54] Firefly employs filtering software that tracks the likes and dislikes of members—movies they enjoyed, restaurants they loathed, and the like. It can then make recommendations about new movies, restaurants, and so on, pegged to the particular tastes of the individual member.

In preparing this paper, I interviewed 35 college students who described themselves as regular users of Internet chat rooms or commercial online services such as AOL.[55] More than two-thirds of them (26) described their conversations with one or more persons as "intimate." More than half (19) reported spending one or more hours a day in some form of online conversation (including e-mail). One had met in person an Internet acquaintance. All 35 (a group self-described as "junkies") rated their online Internet conversations as "important." Six participated in forums with civic, religious, environmental, or political content; the rest were talking pop-cultural topics such as movies, Broadway shows, travel, and television.

The marvel of electronic chat is captured in the experiences of Tonya Price, a self-proclaimed *Star Trek* junkie who went looking online for fellow Trekkers she could not find on campus. She found company on the World Wide Web and on AOL.[56] On AOL, Price ended up talking not to all manner of Trekkers, but only those interested in the second series, *Star Trek: The Next Generation.* Even this was too big a group; she went looking for conversation about the series' concept of *imzadi* (roughly translated as one's "soulmate") as expressed in the relationship between two of the show's regular characters. Eventually, she found about 15 people with whom she began conversations about imzadi.[57] The conversations grew to about an hour a day and culminated in a jointly produced would-be script for the series.[58] In our interview,[59] Price emphasized that she frequently felt more attached to her *Star Trek* community than to her own college classmates, among whom she had never found even one person familiar with the concept of imzadi. Moreover, she described a tight-knit community divided into lurkers and workers, with workers sorted out into writers and editors, all working collaboratively.

The same kind of pinpointed conversation was true of the two students who chatted about Broadway shows. One was "obsessed" (her word) with *The Phantom of the Opera*; the other only wanted to talk about *Rent.* Each found an appropriate chat room and never crossed the virtual street to "visit" each other's favorite show.[60]

I hasten to emphasize that these interviews were of my own students and based on wholly nonrandom selection methods. But the interviews provide anecdotal evidence for two hypotheses about virtual community on the Internet. First is the observation that these communities are frequently self-absorbed by one and only one issue of concern. While this may well provide intense intimacy when members are discussing *Star Trek* or *Rent*, it leaves each a stranger to the rest on all other matters. The *Star Trek* chat room provided an extreme illustration of this phenomenon. Not only did this virtual community exclude from the conversations virtually everything outside of the *Star Trek* universe, the group itself splintered into factions that didn't talk to one another, each one dwelling only on its micro-interest. I understand the thrill a person must feel when she suddenly stumbles upon a whole group of persons who share her passion for episodes of *Star Trek* that mention imzadi. But the thrill is narrow, distracting from social and political concerns, and builds no bridge to involvement in wider forms of community collaboration. (Perhaps this criticism is too harsh. Rheingold's book emphasizes the merit of the World Wide Web in providing links among virtual communities. No matter what Web site I visit these days, I am likely to be guided to other sites and other conversations on allied topics. In this way, the Internet works to build contacts among otherwise separate communities.)

A second hypothesis about virtual community is that it is more likely to revolve around cultural than political issues. Since my sample included only college students, the data may reflect only the preferences of the young. But political life translates poorly into virtual reality. French philosopher Jean-Jacques Rousseau criticized theatergoers for sitting in the dark and feeling pity for imaginary characters in a play when they could be expressing their sympathy through the hard work of helping their actual fellow citizens. So it seems with virtual community. It is far easier to belong virtually to a group which does not expect its meetings to produce action in the real world (no one in the *Phantom of the Opera* chat room thought that their chat was going to change the show) than to a group that meets in order to act, as political groups do. Because conversations in virtual space seem so distant from the possibility of action, they are not the best possible platform for reengaging citizens with their local governing institutions.

(In this regard, however, it is interesting to take note of experiments in empowering virtual communities. For instance, from the earliest days of the Fox Network's television show *The X-Files*, the show's script writers, producers, and others, would monitor, and occasionally join, devoted viewers in a chat room on Delphi right after the airing of each show. The staff of the show have said that these "X-philes" have indeed influenced the content of the show.)

Pornography presents another set of problems to the ideal of free, unregulated, self-governing communities in cyberspace. In 1997, the U.S. Supreme Court struck down the Communications Decency Act as an overbroad attempt to regulate access of minors to indecent sexual material.[61] But this makes it only more imperative for the Net to police itself. On Usenet alone, forty-two separate sex discussion groups exist.

Yet virtual community should be given its due. For many it ends geographical or social or spiritual isolation by bringing kindred spirits together across obstacles of space and time. Perhaps most importantly, individuals gain the experience of creating and governing their own communities. Analyzing the "homesteading" and "pioneering" metaphors, Rheingold documents the excitement generated over the Net as people accustomed to passivity take on the responsibilities of active citizenship in building their own communities.

CONCLUSION

As of this writing, no one knows where these new forms of electronic engagement will take us. Perhaps people whose Internet intimacy starts with *Star Trek* will grow to share broader, more directly political concerns. Or perhaps they will journey further into the virtual heavens, following the example of last year's Heaven's Gate group. The only certain conclusion is that technology itself does not determine the values, the choices, the ideals around which people build their communities.

ENDNOTES

1. Amy Cortese, "A Census in Cyberspace," *Business Week*, 5 May 1997, 85.
2. Paul Curtis, "Not a Highway But a Place," *CPSR [Computer Professionals for Social Responsibility] Newsletter*, Fall 1994.
3. Robert D. Hof, Seanna Browder, and Peter Elstrom, "Internet Communities," *Business Week*, 5 May 1997, 64, 66.
4. Ibid., 66.
5. Ibid., 68.
6. Cortese, "A Census in Cyberspace," 85.
7. Ibid.
8. Hof, Browder, and Elstrom, "Internet Communities," 66.
9. Richard Korman, "Inventing It: Faith and Doubt for a Maker of Modems," *New York Times*, 17 August 1997, sec. 3, p. 7.

10. Cortese, "A Census in Cyberspace," 85.
11. See, for example, GardenEscape at http://www.birdsalldesigns.com/home_ pgs/Garden_Escape/, Parent Soup at http://www.parentsoup.com/, Tripod (twentysomething chat) at http://www.tripod.com/, Women's Wire at http://www. women.com/, and Agriculture Online at http://www.agriculture.com/.
12. When the 1997 Harris/Baruch College poll asked users which term ("social," "professional," or "hobby") best described the online community in which they most frequently participated, 42 percent of respondents selected "professional group," 35 percent selected "social group," and only 18 percent characterized their online communities as united by a hobby. Cortese, "A Census in Cyberspace," 85.
13. See GolfWeb at http://services.golfweb.com/ and Utne Online at http://www. utne.com/.
14. Hof, Browder, and Elstrom, "Internet Communities," 60. See PlanetOut at http://www.planetout.com/.
15. Hof, Browder, and Elstrom, "Internet Communities," 60.
16. See, for example, Michael Dertouzos, *What Will Be: How the New World of Information Technologies Will Change Our Lives* (New York: HarperEdge, 1997); and Howard Rheingold, *Virtual Communities: Homesteading on the Electronic Frontier* (New York: Harper Perennial, 1993).
17. Michael Sandel, *Democracy's Discontents: America in Search of a Public Philosophy* (New York: Harvard University Press, 1996).
18. See, for example: Benjamin Barber, *Strong Democracy: Participatory Politics for a New Age* (Berkeley: University of California Press, 1984); Robert Putnam, "The Strange Disappearance of Civic America," *The American Prospect*, Winter 1996; and Michael Sandel, *Democracy's Discontents*.
19. White was quoted in Chris Ready, "Shelving Young Hopes," *Boston Globe*, 30 August 1992, 27.
20. Carmen Siriani and Lewis Friedland, "Civic Innovation and American Democracy," *Change: The Magazine of Higher Learning* (January/February 1997), 14.
21. See, for example, Amitai Etzioni, *New Communitarian Thinking: Persons, Virtues, Institutions, and Communities* (Charlottesville: University Press of Virginia, 1995).
22. Robert Putnam, "Bowling Alone: America's Declining Social Capital," *Journal of Democracy* (January 1995), 65–78.
23. Cortese, "A Census in Cyberspace," 85.
24. See *Star Wars* online at http://www/starwars.com; AOL keyword=Cinema Chat. See the discussion about slavery at slavery@listserv.uh.edu.
25. Contact the juror's rights group at jrights@levellers.org; see them online at http://www/lrt.org/jrp.homepage.htm.
26. See UptoDate at http://www/uptodateinc.com.
27. See the *Star Trek* scriptwriter's collective at http://www/ultranet.com/zlana.
28. See the Seattle Community Network online at http://www.scn.org/.
29. Doug Schuler, *New Community Networks: Wired for Change* (Boston: Addison Wesley, 1996), preface.
30. Ibid., 25.

31. Telnet: freenet-in-a.cwru.edu.
32. Schuler, *New Community Networks*, Appendix C.
33. Santa Monica's Public Electronic Network is available online at http://www.
    ci.santa-monica.ca.us/pen/.
34. See the Civic Practices Network online at http://www.cpn.org.
35. Carmen Siriani, personal interview with author, 3 May 1997.
36. Carmen Siriani, Lewis Friedland, and Melissa Bass, "The Civic Practices
    Network: Social Learning for a New Citizenship," *The CPSR Newsletter* (Summer
    1996), 1–7.
37. See, for example, links to the Pew Center for Civic Journalism at http://www.
    cpn.org/sections/affiliates/pew.html and the Center for Democracy and Citizenship
    at http://www.cpn.org/sections/affiliates/cdc.html. See the Morino Institute at
    http://www.cpn.org/sections/affiliates/morino.html, the National Civic League at
    http://www.cpn.org/sections/affiliates/ncl.html, and the Kettering Foundation at
    http://www.cpn.org/sections/affiliates/kettering.html.
38. Siriani, personal interview.
39. Margaret Wertheim, "Virtually Heaven?" *Metropolis*, November 1996, 47–50.
40. Korman, "Inventing It."
41. For more information about global Internet "haves" and "have-nots," see Heather
    Hudson's contribution to this volume.
42. Benton Foundation and Libraries for the Future, *Local Places, Global
    Connections: Libraries in the Digital Age* (Washington, D.C.: Communications
    Development Incorporated, 1997), 14–42. See Charlotte's Web at
    http://www.charweb.org/ and the Public Library of Charlotte and Mecklenburg
    County, North Carolina, at http://www.plcmc.lib.nc.us/. See the Cleveland Public
    Electronic Library at http:\\www.cpl.org. See the People for Puget Sound at
    http:\\www.puget-sound.org and the Seattle Public Library at http:\\www.
    spl.lib.wa.us. See the California State Library's Internet for People project at
    http://www.lib.berkeley.edu:8000/. See Nebraska@Online at http://www.nol.org.
43. Benton Foundation, *Local Places, Global Connections*, 4.
44. See the Center for Neighborhood Technology at http://www.cnt.org/.
45. See the Seattle Community Network's Lesbian Gay Bisexual Transgender
    Community at http://www.scn.org/people/gbt.general; its Alcoholics Anonymous
    forum at http://www/scn.org/civic/crisis/dependency/html; and postings for after-
    school clubs at http://www.scn.org/edu/wmsptsa/after-school.fs.html.
46. See the Taos La Plaza telecommunity online at http://www.laplaza.org/. See its
    various fora at http://www.laplaza.org/about_lap/lists_at_lap.html or majordomo
    @laplaza.org.
47. Kent Jones, personal interview with author, Babson College, Wellesley, Mass., 21
    July 1997.
48. Thomas J. Meyer, "No Sound Bite Here," *New York Times Magazine*, 15 March
    1992, sec. 6, p. 46.
49. Rheingold, *Virtual Community*, chapters two and three generally.
50. See the WELL online at http://www.well.com/.
51. Hof, Browder, and Elstrom, "Internet Communities," 65.

52. Dinty W. Moore, *The Emperor's Virtual Clothes: The Naked Truth About Internet Culture* (Chapel Hill: Algonquin Books, 1995), 87–88.
53. See ECHO online at http://www.echonyc.com/; see the Spring at http://www.spring.com/.
54. See the Firefly Network at http://www.firefly.com/.
55. Interviews with 35 college students, 29–30 April 1997.
56. See *Star Trek* on the Web at http://www/co.uk/GreatLink, and AOL's *Star Trek* Club (keyword=Star Trek).
57. See the imzadi message folder in the AOL *Star Trek* Club.
58. See the imzadi *Star Trek* script at http://www/ultranet.com/zlana.
59. Tonya Price, personal interview with author, 29 April 1997.
60. Personal interviews with author, 30 April 1997.
61. *Reno v ACLU*, 117 S Ct, 2329 (1997).

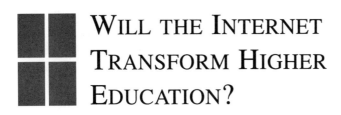

WILL THE INTERNET TRANSFORM HIGHER EDUCATION?

Walter S. Baer

Senior Policy Analyst
RAND Corporation

American higher education faces formidable challenges caused by changing student demographics, severe financial constraints, and lingering institutional rigidities.[1] At the same time, increased demands are being placed on higher education to provide greater student access to education, better undergraduate programs, and increased productivity. To address both sets of issues, institutions of higher education are turning to new communications and information technologies that promise to increase access, improve the quality of instruction, and (perhaps) control costs.

Older technologies for distance learning in post-secondary education[2] have already been shown to be cost-effective in such diverse settings as the Open University in the United Kingdom, four-year and community colleges in the United States, satellite-delivered video courses for engineers and other professionals, and corporate and military training. Now the Internet is being proposed as the preferred technology to improve instruction, increase access, and raise productivity in higher education.[3] College and university instructors now routinely post their syllabi and course readings to the World Wide Web. A few use lectures and other instructional materials available on the Web in their own courses. A growing number of schools offer at least some extension or degree-credit courses over the Internet. And more ambitious plans are in various stages of preparation or early implementation—plans for entire *virtual universities* that use the Internet to reach geographically dispersed students.

Two distinct models guide current efforts to make use of the Internet in higher education. The first approach seeks to improve existing forms and structures of post-secondary instruction—to create "better, faster, cheaper" versions of today's courses and curricula by means of the Internet. This model emphasizes building an on-campus information infrastructure that provides (or will provide) high-speed Internet connectivity to all students, faculty, administrators, and staff. Faculty then can use this infrastructure to improve and supplement traditional courses and degree programs. Library holdings can be digitized and made available both on- and off-campus.[4] Administrative processes can be speeded up and simplified. And although the focus remains on on-campus instruction, this new information infrastructure can facilitate distance learning for many categories of nontraditional, off-campus students. While this model of Internet use in higher education requires many changes among faculty, student, and administrative roles and functions, it keeps most existing institutional structures and faculty roles intact.

A different, more radical, model envisions the Internet as instrumental to a fundamental change in the processes and organizational structure of post-secondary teaching and learning. According to this view, the Internet can transform higher education into student-centered learning rather than institution- and faculty-centered instruction. It can allow agile institutions—old and new—to leapfrog existing academic structures and establish direct links to post-secondary students. It can encourage new collaborative arrangements between academic institutions and for-profit entrepreneurs and permit these partnerships to extend their reach nationally and internationally. It can accommodate student demand for post-secondary education in new ways that are basically campus-independent. If the markets for post-secondary education evolve in this manner, the Internet may well threaten existing institutions of higher education much more than it will support them. Taking this view, celebrated management consultant and social commentator Peter Drucker recently remarked: "Thirty years from now the big university campuses will be relics. . . . The college won't survive as a residential institution."[5]

This chapter explores these two conflicting views of the Internet's evolving role in higher education. The discussion begins with an introduction to a number of academic projects that use the Internet for both on-campus instruction and distance learning.[6] The chapter then examines the ways in which private-sector firms are using the Internet for training and education, giving special attention to the firms' plans to cooperate or compete with academic institutions. The chapter concludes with a discussion of important issues raised by the Internet's expansion into higher education and the implications of this expansion for students, faculty, and academic institutions.

THE INTERNET ON CAMPUS

Although U.S. universities pioneered the development of the Internet and employed it for scholarly research in the 1970s and 1980s, its application to undergraduate and graduate instruction has occurred mainly in this decade. This extension of the Internet's educational function has brought about both a rapid expansion of the campus information infrastructure and an ongoing struggle with the financial and other difficulties inherent in the adoption of new technologies.

Expanding the Campus Information Infrastructure

American colleges and universities are investing heavily today to upgrade their computer systems, local area networks, and Internet links. More than fifty schools—ranging from community colleges to large research universities—have joined in the National Learning Infrastructure Initiative, a consortium created "to facilitate technology-mediated learning" on the nation's campuses.[7]

On American campuses, the Internet is now used primarily to supplement face-to-face lectures and other classroom activities, and to make course materials available for students' use at times of their own choosing. Common applications include: placing course outlines, syllabi, readings, and assignments on the Web; encouraging students to gather course-related information from the Web and submit papers and other assignments by electronic mail; engaging in one-on-one, student-faculty discussions via e-mail (a practice sometimes known as *virtual office hours*); and holding larger class discussions via e-mail. These applications are becoming widespread on campuses; the University of Illinois at Urbana-Champaign's Web site alone lists nearly 250 "classes with Web resources."[8] The 1997 Campus Computing Survey reports that nearly one-third of college courses now use electronic mail, up from twenty percent in 1995.[9]

People who argue for use of the Internet to make on-campus instruction more student-centered and inquiry-based offer visions that feature entire courses held on the Internet, complete with lectures and multimedia presentations available on-demand or *asynchronously*; student access to fully digital libraries and information sources; interactive simulations of complex phenomena and real-world situations; Internet-based videoconferences with the leading scholars in a given field; and collaborative projects among students and experts from around the world. Demonstrations of such concepts are under way at a large number of colleges and universities.[10]

Cost and Other Obstacles to On-Campus Internet Instruction

But the Internet has not yet brought about major changes in on-campus instruction. It is still too new, too costly, and perhaps too threatening to existing academic structures and traditions.

High start-up costs for on-campus networks and Internet-based instruction certainly pose problems. Many schools have been caught relatively unprepared for the heavy Internet usage of students who now come to college experienced in using computers and the Internet at home, in secondary school, or in summer or part-time jobs.[11] These undergraduates have high expectations for improving their computer skills and applying those skills directly in their course work. Their usage demands have brought some campus computer networks to their knees and forced administrators to ration Internet availability.[12] The provision of student access to computer networks, once considered a marginal add-on to the cost of research computing, now requires a large and growing budget of its own.

Developing new course materials for the Internet can also involve substantial initial costs, particularly of faculty time. While it is now relatively easy to put documents and other text on the Web, much of the Internet's power as a learning medium lies both in integrating relevant visual, aural, and textual materials and in providing access to these materials in nonlinear ways. Doing this well requires a good deal of instructor time, thought, and effort. In many cases it will also require support in the course-design phase from multimedia experts, support that few academic institutions today are able to provide.

One approach to dealing with the development-cost problem is to assemble courses using already-built instructional modules. The "World Lecture Hall" at the University of Texas and "Archive.edu" at the University of Houston, among other projects, are collecting and cataloging online courses and course modules and making them available free to other instructors.[13] As an illustration, the World Lecture Hall indexes and links to about fifty courses on economics, such as this course on Intermediate Microeconomics from the University of Delaware:

> Multimedia Web site with over seventy Java applets. Integrated textbook, lecture series, graphical calculator, animated drawing program, spreadsheet, and econometrics package. Lecture notes.[14]

The availability of such materials for downloading at no cost can in principle reduce the costs of preparing and delivering Web-based courses. However, instructors must already be familiar with the Internet to make use of the materials, and even Net-savvy faculty must spend considerable time reviewing materials and deciding how to incorporate them into their own courses. There are as yet no peer-review mechanisms for evaluating Internet curricular materials. And although instructors commonly use textbooks written by others, most are not ready to substitute multimedia course modules prepared elsewhere for their own on-campus lectures.

The basic concept of making the best presentations by the world's leading authorities widely available over the Internet will seem job-threatening to some who fear that administrators, trustees, and/or state legislators, in their zeal to reduce costs, will see the Internet as a substitute for live instruction. Not a complete substitute, of course—face-to-face contact between faculty and students is still the essence of high-quality on-campus instruction, and seems likely to remain so for the foreseeable future. But live lectures to hundreds of students in introductory courses could be especially vulnerable to replacement by Internet-based, multimedia presentations from Nobel-prize winners or charismatic lecturers. The argument that this could in fact free up faculty time for more effective interaction with students in smaller groups has not yet been very persuasive in changing traditional teaching patterns.

Such concerns about technology's impact on teaching are not confined to the Internet, of course; the same possibilities and problems were raised fifty years ago with instructional television, and more recently with personal computers and multimedia CD-ROMs. With a few exceptions such as the Rensselaer Polytechnic Institute "studio courses,"[15] television and computers have had only marginal effects on instruction and have not led to improvements in productivity. Like these technologies, the Internet must overcome the innate conservatism of academia and a host of institutional obstacles if it is to become more than a supplementary, cost-additive element of on-campus instruction.

THE INTERNET'S ROLE IN DISTANCE LEARNING

Distance learning is an increasingly important focus for educational institutions, which are struggling with the concept, weighing its advantages and disadvantages, and planning and executing pilot projects to test its effectiveness.

What is Distance Learning?

The concept of distance learning—that is, education and training off-campus or away from the source of instruction and information—goes back at least to the nineteenth century, when both academic and for-profit institutions began to offer correspondence courses by mail. Each technology for electronic delivery of information has subsequently been used for distance learning: the telephone; radio; broadcast, cable, and satellite television; audiotapes, videotapes, and videodisks; audio- and videoconferencing; timesharing on mainframe computers; PC software and CD-ROMs; and now the Internet.[16]

Distance learning is generally associated with part-time or "non-traditional" post-secondary students, particularly those who want to increase their job-related knowledge and skills. Some seek formal undergraduate or graduate degrees, while others enroll in classes leading to continuing-education credits, certificates of completion, or similar certification. Still others engage in distance learning for personal fulfillment rather than to obtain credits or credentials. Moreover, the potential market for distance learning includes such heterogeneous groups as:

- full-time students temporarily off-campus because of illness, work, or travel
- on-campus students who want to take classes from another institution
- people working full- or part-time
- military service personnel and their dependents
- parents at home with small children
- people living far away from educational centers
- prisoners
- retirees and others not actively working

In 1995, according to U.S. government and industry data, more than seventy-five million American adults, or about forty percent of all adults, participated in some part-time educational program. And part-time enrollment in higher education is growing more than three times faster than full-time enrollment.[17]

Most U.S. colleges and universities offer some distance-learning courses, usually through separate extension or continuing-education divisions that employ part-time, nontenured instructors. Many community colleges, state colleges, and universities, and other schools that emphasize teaching, have extensive distance-learning programs focused on part-time students who can receive course credits and earn degrees off-campus. But even elite research universities are competing more aggressively to offer continuing-education classes to professionals, as they begin to recognize that distance learning offers a separate and growing revenue stream to financially strapped institutions, and begin to take steps so as not to be left out.[18]

Is Distance Learning Effective?

Numerous studies over the past several decades generally conclude that distance learning works and is cost-effective in imparting knowledge across a wide range of subjects to diverse categories of students.[19] Students who complete courses off-site typically learn as much and score as well on examinations as those who attend class in person. The costs for distance learning are nearly always lower, often by fifty percent or more, than those of on-campus classes. Moreover, in most cases the technology used to deliver distance learning does not appear to be particularly crucial to its success. Most studies find no significant differences in student learning for courses taught using different media technologies.[20]

However, it takes more motivation to pursue classes on one's own than in a group setting, and thus completion rates can be much lower for distance learning than for classroom courses. For this reason, institutions providing distance learning often build in faculty-student and group discussions via telephone, audio- or videoconferencing, or (preferably) face-to-face meetings. The Open University in the United Kingdom, a world leader in distance learning for more than twenty-five years, finds such interactions essential to student success and schedules face-to-face tutorials as an integral part of each distance-learning course.

Still, distance learning is clearly less effective than time spent on-campus in helping students form academic relationships, business networks, and friendships. These benefits are less readily measurable than test results but very important to career and personal success. As John Seely Brown and Paul Duguid point out in a recent article, "People leave college knowing not just things, but knowing people, and knowing not just academic facts, but knowing social strategies for dealing with the world. Reliable friendships and complex social structures aren't picked up through lectures, but they give an education much of its value."[21]

Advantages and Disadvantages of the Internet for Distance Learning

Compared with other media for distance learning, the Internet offers more interactivity, greater flexibility, more functionality, and potentially lower costs:

- *Interactivity.* The Internet is inherently a two-way medium that facilitates both one-to-one and group communication, both in real time and asynchronously. Much of the educational promise of the Internet lies in its ability to foster interactive *learning communities* in which participants routinely exchange information, debate course topics, and build relationships through informal discussion and social chat. This interactive capability addresses the chief weakness of other distance-learning media that are either one-way (print materials, radio and television, audio- and videotapes, computer software and CD-ROMs), or cumbersome and expensive for group discussions (audio- and videoconferencing). Internet communication today is principally via e-mail, but the software for voice messaging and real-time conversation is diffusing rapidly, and two-way video will likely be available and affordable within the next five years.

- *Flexibility.* The Internet provides on-demand access to course materials and discussions at the student's preferred time and place. Information and messages can easily be sent to an individual or shared with the entire class. Course materials or links to other sites can be rapidly updated and made available to all participants simultaneously. Students and instructors also can exchange information and communicate using different equipment, which is generally not possible on other proprietary computer networks.

- *Functionality.* Through the Internet, students can have ready access to image and audio, as well as text materials. Today, the low data rates available using standard telephone lines and modems make extensive use of full-motion video impractical, but new digital compression and transmission technologies over telephone and cable networks should reduce these bottlenecks within the next five to ten years.[22]

- *Cost and access.* For academic institutions, providing instructional materials on the Internet should be less expensive than delivering the same materials through the mail or over broadcast media. For students, usage costs are quite low once they have obtained Internet access, particularly compared with using other interactive media such as audio- or videoconferencing. However, the initial costs of acquiring a computer, an Internet connection, and (especially) the skills to use them effectively present barriers for many students. These barriers are decreasing over time as more people own computers and become familiar with the Internet, but they nevertheless will pose constraints on Internet distance learning for at least the next decade.[23]

Current Use of the Internet for Distance Learning

A great many academic institutions that offer distance learning are using or experimenting with the Internet for off-campus instructional delivery. Some interesting examples:

- The Open University, a long-time leader in distance learning, is only now beginning to offer instruction via the Internet.[24] The Open University's record of success is based on supplementing individual self-study with feedback from assigned tutors via mail, telephone, and face-to-face tutorials. Currently, only three computing courses (out of more than three hundred courses available) use the Internet. Students in these courses can submit assignments, communicate with their tutors, and participate in some tutorials via e-mail. Most course materials (including paper documents, audiotapes, and videotapes) are still sent by mail, and students must attend the final examination in person. The Internet courses are targeted to "those who live far away from our study centres in the UK, Ireland, and Continental Western Europe or whose employment or domestic situation makes it difficult for them to travel to a study centre."[25]

- The California State University (CSU) system is making a major effort to use the Internet for graduate, undergraduate, and non-degree distance learning.[26] As an example, CSU–Dominguez Hills offers a fully accredited graduate degree program—the Master of Science in Quality Assurance (MSQA)—over the Internet. More than fifty students from the United States and seven other countries are enrolled in MSQA On-Line, "a series of Web sites that allow students to download the student handbook, review course syllabi, register for courses, attend lectures, do their assignments, use resources, participate in class discussions, network with other students, and communicate with their professors."[27] CSU–Sonoma State has designed a Composite B.A. Degree Program in Liberal Studies for students who have completed their first two years of general education. Students enrolling in this program must attend classes on campus one Saturday per month, but they otherwise participate via the Internet. And (as discussed later in this chapter), CSU–Long Beach is working with a for-profit firm, UOL Publishing, Inc., to offer courses on the Internet leading to a

Certificate in Planned Giving.[28] Overall, by the end of 1997, eighteen of the twenty-three CSU campuses were offering online courses.[29]

- Two leading campuses of the University of California have joined with for-profit firms to offer extension courses over the Internet. UCLA Extension is collaborating with the Home Education Network; currently about a thousand students in forty-four states and eight countries are enrolled in some fifty courses taught over the Internet.[30] UC–Berkeley Extension is working with America Online to offer about forty online courses.[31] UC–Berkeley Extension and UOL Publishing, Inc., have also signed an agreement to develop and distribute over the Internet, beginning in fall 1997, seven marketing courses leading to a Certificate in Marketing.[32]

- Duke University's Fuqua School of Business offers a Global Executive M.B.A. program by e-mail over the Internet. Nearly half of those enrolled in this new program live outside the United States.[33]

- Park College, which focuses on undergraduate degree completion programs for U.S. military service enlistees and their dependents, has made a strong commitment to using the Internet for distance learning. Begun on a trial basis in 1996, Park College Online now offers more than twenty degree-credit courses over the Internet in biology, chemistry, computer science, criminal justice, English, history, management, marketing, and social psychology.[34]

- Virginia Commonwealth University (VCU) and the Medical College of Virginia (MCV) offer an Executive Masters Program in Health Administration that combines on-campus with Internet-based instruction.[35] During the two-year program, students attend five one- to two-week sessions at the MCV campus in Richmond, Virginia; they complete the rest of their course work off site using e-mail and the World Wide Web.

"Virtual Universities"

The concept of the virtual university involves broader and more ambitious goals than other distance-learning programs. As the term is used here, the core mission of a virtual university is to offer complete academic degree programs—and usually non-degree courses as well—on the Internet to students who are widely dispersed geographically. Student presence on-campus is not required to earn course credits or degrees, although (like several of the distance-learning examples described above) virtual universities may want to supplement electronic tutorials and group discussions with some face-to-face interactions. Virtual universities will still use books and other instructional media such as audio- or videotapes and software/CD-ROMs, but their central focus is on interactive learning via the Internet.

While a variety of academic and non-academic programs use the terms "virtual university" or "virtual campus" to describe themselves, the following appear to be among the most comprehensive examples:

- The Western Governors' University was announced in December 1995 when the governors of eleven Western states agreed to explore the creation of a virtual university.[36] The Western Governors' University expects to become operational in early 1998. As currently envisioned, the Western Governors' University will be an independent, nonprofit, accredited, degree-granting entity drawing on faculty from other public and private institutions in the region to teach courses using the Internet and other distance-learning technologies. It will emphasize practical competency-based degrees and certification, rather than traditional academic credits earned by what is called "seat-time." "Market-oriented" and "client-centered, focusing [on] the needs of students and employers,"[37] it will offer an Associate of Arts degree and certification for electronic technicians. It will also broker distance-learning courses for other participating institutions.

- International University was founded in 1995 by Glenn Jones, a communications and higher-education entrepreneur, to provide Internet-based undergraduate and graduate "degree courses, non-credit courses, certificates of specialization, and degree programs."[38] International University offers both a B.A. completion program (for students who have two to three years of undergraduate credits from another institution) and an M.A. in Business Communications, as well as certificates of specialization in that field. No degrees have been awarded as yet, but the school has been granted candidacy status for accreditation by the North Central Association of Colleges and Schools. International University's focus on online delivery complements other of Jones' enterprises that employ broadcast television, cable, satellite, videotape, software, and CD-ROM technologies for distance learning.

- Athena University, a nonprofit subsidiary of Virtual Online University, Inc., provides interactive, Internet-based courses that diverge further from traditional academic offerings than the other distance-learning examples cited in this section. Athena's instructional delivery model "is constructed on an Internet program called a Multi-User, Object Oriented (MOO) environment,"[39] in which faculty and students can interact with each other as "cyber-objects" as well as exchange messages and information. Athena intends to offer both an undergraduate liberal arts degree and an M.B.A. in New Technologies for New Management Strategies, and is seeking accreditation from the North Central Association of Colleges and Schools.

PRIVATE-SECTOR INTERESTS IN INTERNET-BASED EDUCATION

Private-sector firms have several distinct roles to play in Internet-based post-secondary education and training: as vendors of hardware and software; as system developers, system integrators, and publishers; as commercial providers of corporate training; as consumers of employee training and education; and as operators of for-profit, degree-granting institutions.

Hardware and Software Vendors

Higher education is an important market for vendors of telecommunications and information systems hardware and software. It is in these firms' direct interest to work closely with academic administrators and faculty on plans to upgrade the campus information infrastructure and expand distance learning. As one example, the League for Innovation in the Community Colleges receives considerable support for its Information Technology Initiative from more than fifty "corporate partners" including Apple Computer, IBM, Microsoft, Oracle, and U.S. Robotics.[40] And Silicon Graphics and Sun Microsystems, not surprisingly, are among the sponsors of Web-based courses on Structure-Based Drug Design and Bioinformatics Tools offered by the Department of Pharmaceutical Sciences at the University of Nottingham.[41]

System Developers and Publishers

Many companies view Internet-based education as a growth market and are positioning themselves to serve it. Two leading examples are IBM and UOL Publishing, Inc.

IBM. In October 1996, IBM announced its Global Campus, described as "a breakthrough education and business framework that helps colleges and universities use computer networks to redesign learning, teaching, and administrative functions."[42] Still under development, the IBM Global Campus will provide a common software and administrative framework—using Lotus Notes and other IBM products—for Web-based courses offered by participating university and college "affiliates." The initial affiliates include all twenty-three campuses of the California State University system and thirty-two other colleges and universities in the U.S., Australia, Canada, Mexico, Brazil, and Venezuela.

IBM will not develop courseware for the Global Campus itself (at least for now), but it plans to offer technical and administrative services to both students and educational institutions, ranging from Internet access to course registration to online student discussion groups. IBM will also facilitate the development and sharing of authoring tools, instructional modules, and online catalogs for Internet-delivered courses. The IBM Global Campus is both an ambitious future-oriented concept for Internet-based instruction and a focused marketing campaign to sell Lotus Notes software, "Domino" Web servers, and other IBM products to the higher-education sector.

UOL Publishing, Inc. A relatively new company, UOL is positioning itself as a publisher and distributor of courses on the Internet for both academic institutions and business firms.[43] UOL will either commission development of courseware for Internet delivery, like a traditional publisher, or partner with institutions that develop their own courses. It will then market the courses to other institutions, with current licensing fees of about $100 per student per course. The courses will be available on UOL's Web server, and UOL will also provide administrative services (including registration, grading, accounting, and reporting) on a turnkey basis for participating institutions.

UOL Publishing's initial group of academic partners is mostly offering certificate and other non-degree programs, or pilot-testing courses for degree credit. As examples:

- CSU–Long Beach offers a Certified Specialist in Planned Giving Program through its University College and Extension Program.[44] The program consists of six modules, the first two of which are available online from UOL Publishing. Students complete the remaining four modules on the CSU–Long Beach campus.

- Georgetown University School of Business gives a certificate to students who complete an online course in International Business through UOL.[45]

- George Mason University (GMU) offers two online courses, one in Financial Accounting and one in Managerial Statistics, both of which can be taken for degree credit in the GMU Graduate Business Institute.[46]

Other UOL Publishing academic partners include George Washington University, New York University, Park College, the University of Toledo, and Xavier University.

Overall, UOL Publishing's business plan to create, market, and distribute online courses in partnership with academic institutions seems well-thought out, and its initial focus on extension and certificate courses seems realistic in the current environment. Whether UOL's course offerings can move into the degree-granting academic mainstream, however, remains to be seen.

Commercial Providers and Users of Corporate Education and Training

Corporate education and training in the United States represents a $50 billion annual business that is forecast to grow steadily as companies invest in their human capital for competitive advantage in global markets.[47] Although computer-based training will not replace instructor-led, classroom training for many applications, both commercial providers of training and corporate users see Internet- and Intranet-based instruction as productivity-enhancing tools. In particular, Web-based training can follow initial classroom training; and it can be taken at the employee's convenience, often outside of normal working hours. It thus can significantly reduce the travel costs and paid staff time that would otherwise be spent on additional classroom training.

Software firms are among the leaders in experimenting with Internet- and Intranet-delivered instruction:

- After about two years of testing Web-based training, Microsoft is now aggressively promoting it through its Microsoft Online Institute (MOLI).[48] Microsoft provides the Web infrastructure and administrative services, but the actual courses are developed and offered by third-party training organizations whose content has been approved by Microsoft. The focus is on training information technology specialists to use Microsoft products; a student can become a Microsoft Certified Professional through online instruction. Microsoft is also encouraging its classroom-based Authorized Technical Education Centers (ATECs) to set up parallel Internet training through MOLI.

- Oracle, the second largest software company, also has established an Internet-based training environment called Oracle Learning Architecture (OLA).[49] Like Microsoft, Oracle's initial market is professionals whom it trains to use the company's products, but Oracle intends to expand OLA to serve a far broader range of corporate training applications.

- Novell Education trains and certifies administrators, instructors, and engineers in the use of Novell software products. Novell is actively pursuing asynchronous, Web-based training to supplement and partially substitute for the 750,000 student courses taken each year in instructor led, classroom training.[50]

- Autodesk, a leading supplier of PC-based design software, has established its Autodesk Virtual Campus in partnership with UOL Publishing to offer courses in computer aided design over the Internet.[51] The Autodesk Virtual Campus also provides technical support, discussion groups, and job listings. Autodesk and UOL are partnering with a number of other firms to develop content for specific courses.

Most other commercial training providers are planning to deliver or at least are considering providing courses over the Internet. As one example, Dun & Bradstreet Information Services now conducts a Web-based training seminar to teach customers how to use the DIALOG information retrieval service, the first of many training seminars it hopes to offer online.[52] Although up to now, Web-based corporate training has focused on computer-related topics and skills, the widespread corporate use of Internet and Intranet sites will inevitably carry Web-based training with it into other, nontechnical areas.

For-Profit, Degree-Granting Institutions

Although proprietary trade schools have been an important segment of post-secondary education for many years, for-profit entities generally have not been accredited for granting undergraduate or graduate degrees. One interesting exception is the University of Phoenix, a for-profit subsidiary of Apollo Group, Inc., which is accredited to grant bachelor's and master's degrees by the North Central Association of Colleges and Schools.[53] Founded in 1976, the University of Phoenix focuses on providing practical degree programs for working adults. With forty thousand students enrolled on more than fifty campuses, it has become the largest private university in the United States.[54]

The University of Phoenix began testing asynchronous, computer-based instruction in 1989 and now has some twenty-six hundred students enrolled in its online degree programs.[55] Online students usually are older than on-campus students (late thirties to early forties) and have previously earned some college credits from another institution. On average, they take slightly more than 100 online course credits in two-and-one-half to three years to complete the requirements for a Bachelor's degree in Business. The individual online course- and degree-completion rates are an impressive ninety-three percent and sixty percent, respectively,[56] about the same as those for successful on-campus programs. The University of Phoenix also offers, via the Internet, continuing professional education courses with Certificates of Completion.

DISCUSSION

As the previous sections of this chapter have indicated, information technology in general and the Internet in particular show real potential in post-secondary education for improving instructional quality, student access, and productivity. There are, of course, tradeoffs among these goals, but experience from process reengineering in industry suggests that all three can and should be addressed simultaneously. Foremost among the important issues are questions of instructional cost, student access, the relationship between the private sector and academia, and the impact of the Internet on education.

The Instructional Cost Problem

Most efforts to date to use the Internet in higher education have concentrated on the goals of improving quality and student access. Improving productivity by reducing instructional cost has played a lesser role, for a variety of reasons:

- Existing courses cannot simply be transplanted onto the Internet. Developing courseware for Internet delivery requires a considerable investment of faculty time that typically brings scant monetary or professional rewards.

- Enthusiasts usually discount the amount of human support needed for effective PC- or Internet-based learning. Such underestimates are consistent with business experience that annualized PC costs break down roughly into twenty percent hardware and software costs, and eighty percent people costs.

- Research universities have had (at least up to now) little incentive to reduce instructional costs, since they represent a relatively small percentage of overall operating costs.

- State funding for higher education is often based on student on-campus attendance ("seat time"), with institutions receiving less for courses taught using the Internet or other modes of distance learning.

- Faculty may explicitly or implicitly resist changes that they believe threaten their jobs or academic roles.

- Colleges and universities have relatively little control over faculty labor costs, at least in the short run, so information technology usually increases short-run operating costs.

Although there are good reasons to think that Internet-based instruction, used appropriately and effectively, can reduce instructional costs, scant evidence or business modeling exists to support such beliefs.[57] Indeed, some universities currently charge more for online courses than for conventional on-campus classes[58] (although students taking online classes may have lower net costs after considering transportation costs and lost income from traveling to campus). Including productivity/cost improvement as an explicit goal of Internet-based course design seems likely to have significant payoff.

How Quickly Will Colleges and Universities Adopt the Internet?

In light of the breadth and diversity of American higher education, colleges and universities are likely to use the Internet for instruction in quite different ways. Currently the major research universities are embarking on extensive (and expensive) programs to make wideband Internet connectivity ubiquitous on campus. They are driven to do so because they believe it necessary for them to remain competitive for attracting the best students and faculty. Greater use of the Internet should on the whole lead to improved quality of undergraduate and graduate instruction, and to better on-campus administrative services, but it seems unlikely by itself to bring about overall productivity gains. However, a robust campus information infrastructure certainly will support broader restructuring and reengineering efforts that could reduce instructional costs and increase productivity.[59]

Research universities also will seek to broaden access through increased use of Internet-delivered courses to degree and non-degree students off-campus. Although access is not the highest internal priority for most elite institutions, developing new revenue streams from off-campus students is of interest to all of them. University alumni seem a particularly attractive market for Internet-delivered continuing education. Moreover, these institutions' prestige and "brand-name" identification make them attractive partners for commercial firms that offer education and training over the Internet. (This topic is discussed further below.)

Innovative use of the Internet to expand access seems more likely to come from the community colleges and the less-elite colleges and universities.[60] These institutions face severe financial pressures to expand enrollments while reducing per-student costs. Their faculties retain control over courses and curricula, and they are not yet comfortable with the Internet as a core instructional medium, but they seem more amenable than are research-university professors to using course materials prepared by others. Their students also want the kind of practical, job-related education that fits well into a distance-learning paradigm.

Community colleges, state colleges, and other institutions that have well-developed distance-learning programs should generally embrace the Internet as a technologically richer, more flexible, way to reach off-campus students. It seems likely to become a lower-cost medium as well, once courseware and operating procedures are developed; but again there are scant current data to confirm or refute this claim. Problems of providing low-cost equipment and Internet service to rural and low-income students remain, but access is steadily expanding and should accelerate as Universal Service subsidies for school and library Internet services become available in 1998.[61]

Will the Private Sector Compete More Strongly With Academia?

At present, the lines between private-sector and academic providers of post-secondary education and training are still fairly distinct, with the exception of a few boundary-crossing organizations such as the for-profit University of Phoenix. Nevertheless, more confrontations between the two sectors seem likely as the Internet becomes an important teaching and learning platform for nontraditional, mostly off-campus students.

Microsoft, Oracle, and other software companies are building extensive infrastructures for providing their own professional training over the Internet. Once their infrastructures are in place, they will be well-positioned to offer other courses and educational programs to students "anywhere, anytime." They will surely seek institutional academic partners in some areas, as IBM and UOL are doing; but they also can develop courseware independently, like publishers, by hiring individual scholars or practitioners. Microsoft in particular is committed to developing content for the Internet in a publishing-like mode.[62]

Moving from providing infrastructure and publishing courseware to actually offering Web-based courses seems a logical next step. With greater marketing prowess, lower cost structures, and fewer institutional constraints than academic institutions, private firms may be able to use the Internet to compete effectively for students in some areas of non-degree instruction that colleges and universities now dominate, such as:

- remedial courses for entering college students
- extension courses for adults
- professional continuing education
- "short courses" for managers and executives

This line of argument does not suggest that academic institutions are fated to lose out in providing education to non-degree students. Many adults want to come to a physical campus for personal interactions with faculty and students, as well as for instruction. Some classes demand one's physical presence and cannot be taught over the Internet. And outside of purely technical training, certificates or other credits awarded by leading colleges and universities still carry more cachet than those given by commercial firms.

Partnerships between for-profit firms and academic institutions seem the most likely arrangements for offering Internet-based education to non-degree students. But if businesses adapt more rapidly to the new environment and invest more in Internet-based education, they will demand a larger share of the resulting revenue. A quite plausible future scenario would see the commercial partner providing the Internet infrastructure (hardware, software, and communications), much of the course content, administrative services, marketing, and most of the direct contact with students. The academic partner would provide its name on the courses and on the student's Certificate of Completion, as well as take responsibility for student selection, quality control over course content, interactive sessions, and grading.

One clear implication of this scenario is that commercial firms that develop these capabilities will seek out the most prestigious academic partners to offer courses nationally and internationally. In marketing to students, they will have little reason to respect either the geographical or subject-area "turf" of other academic institutions. Such increased competition could put financial pressure on less prestigious schools whose current plans assume substantial revenue from non-degree students. However, such schools can respond competitively by becoming expert in particular content areas (e.g., the Certified Specialist in Planned Giving Program offered online by CSU–Long Beach) and by providing superior services to online students (e.g., real people to talk with when problems arise).

Similar business/academic partnership models also apply to degree-credit courses offered via the Internet, but here the value-added and bargaining position of the academic partners seem stronger. Faculty generally are much more concerned about retaining control over degree programs, so they will want the commercial partner to play a support-ing role. Academics also control the organizations that accredit degree programs. Still, firms should be able to find cooperative and accredited academic partners with whom to offer Internet courses for degree cred-it. This could well become the evolutionary path for virtual universities that offer complete degree programs over the Internet.

Will the Internet Transform Higher Education?

Although any projections of the Internet's future impact should be viewed with skepticism, if not downright alarm, the title of this chapter seems to demand some speculative concluding comments. What fol-lows, though, should be considered more of a scenario than a forecast.

In the near term, most higher-education institutions will use the Internet incrementally to improve administrative processes, on-campus instruction, and distance learning. It will rather quickly become the pre-ferred means to reach off-campus students. But it will be viewed more as a powerful technical tool than as a catalyst for institutional change. "Regulation, bureaucracy, tradition, and turf"[63] will remain barriers to more fundamental academic restructuring, particularly in the elite research universities where faculties have the greatest degree of power and control.

A few academic institutions, spurred by vision or crisis, will seek to reorient instruction toward distributed, student-centered learning with heavy use of Internet-based courseware, discussion groups, and links to other online resources. This seems likely to occur first for con-tinuing education, job-related training, and other non-degree courses, as well as for the expansion of current distance-learning programs. For-profit firms will also move beyond their traditional corporate training markets within the next few years to deliver educational courses more widely via the Internet, often in partnership with academic institutions. Competition for non-degree students will thus become more intense and should lead to lower student costs per course—beginning with

Internet-based classes, but probably then spreading to other modes of instruction.

Degree programs will migrate to the Internet more slowly, although most colleges and universities will soon offer at least some courses online for degree credit. Internet-based virtual universities will provide the lowest-cost degree options, but geography and face-to-face interaction will still play important roles in attracting degree students. Nevertheless, ready availability of courses over the Internet at lower net cost to the student will encourage more off-campus learning. Rather than today's dichotomy between "traditional" and "nontraditional" students, more students will earn degrees by taking a mix of on-campus and Internet-based, off-campus courses. And as competition increases, students will be able to take more Internet courses for credit from sources other than their own degree-granting institution.

Finally, learning from the Internet will complement rather than supplant on-campus traditional higher education. Peter Drucker notwithstanding, one should not expect residential colleges and universities to disappear within a generation. A great many young adults still want the face-to-face instruction and social interactions they get on campus, even if it is more expensive than distance learning. For most secondary-school graduates, the issue will not be choosing between full-time, on-campus study and 100-percent distance learning, but selecting a mix that is educationally sound, accessible, and affordable. In this sense the Internet may not transform higher education, at least for the foreseeable future,[64] but it will enrich the educational choices generally available to all categories of learners.

ENDNOTES

1. While the Internet is a global phenomenon, and innovations on the Internet have global impact, most of the early applications of the Internet to instruction in higher education are occurring in the United States. This article, therefore, mostly focuses on the use of the Internet in American higher education.

2. This chapter uses the terms "higher education" and "post-secondary education" interchangeably. Some might argue that "higher education" should be reserved for degree-granting colleges, universities, and graduate professional schools, and that "higher education" is thus a subset of "post-secondary education," which would also include trade schools, continuing education and other non-degree programs,

and corporate and military training. However, as this chapter argues, the boundaries between the two categories are blurring so that these distinctions will become less meaningful over time.

3. David MacArthur and Matthew Lewis, *Untangling the Web: Applications of the Internet and Other Information Technologies to Higher Education* (Santa Monica, Calif.: RAND, DRU-1401-IET, June 1996).

4. See, for example, Suzanne E. Thorin and Virginia D. Sorkin, "The Library of the Future," in *The Learning Revolution*, ed. Diana G. Oblinger and Sean C. Rush (Bolton, Mass.: Anker Publishing Co., 1997), 164–79.

5. Interview with Peter Drucker, *Forbes*, 10 March 1997. See also similar comments by Eli Noam, "Electronics and the Dim Future of the University," *Science*, 13 October 1995, 247–49.

6. Several Web sites now specialize in tracking such projects and providing direct links to them. See, for example, Cape Software's site, "The Internet University: College Courses by Computer," available online at http://www.caso.com, and the Globewide Network Academy at http://uu-gna.mit.edu:8001/uu-gna/. An annotated compendium, "Learning over the Internet: Courses, Curricula, Programs, Syllabi, etc.," is maintained by Carolyn Kotlas of the Institute for Academic Technology, University of North Carolina, and is available online at http://www.iac.unc.edu/guides/irg-38.html.

7. The National Learning Infrastructure Initiative (NLII) is a project of EDUCOM (http://www.educom.edu), a consortium of colleges that focuses on the use of communications and information technologies in higher education. See "NLII Call to Participate, EDUCOM's National Learning Infrastructure Initiative," November 1994; available online at http://www.educom.edu/program/nlli/keydocs/call.html.

8. The list of "classes with Web resources" at the University of Illinois at Urbana-Champaign is available online at http://www.uiuc.edu/webclasses.html.

9. Kenneth C. Green, "1997 Campus Computing Survey," reported in *The Chronicle of Higher Education*, 17 October 1997.

10. The Alfred P. Sloan Foundation, for example, has given over $15 million in grants since 1993 to more than forty colleges and universities for such projects through its Asynchronous Learning Networks (ALN) program. See the Sloan Web site at http://www.sloan.org/education/ALN.new.html. For an excellent summary of the program by the ALN program director, see A. Frank Mayadas, "Asynchronous Learning Networks: New Possibilities," in *The Learning Revolution*, 211–30.

11. A 1994 survey of high-school graduates of the class of 1990 found that seventy percent of those enrolled in a college or university reported regularly using a computer, compared with fifty-seven percent of those not attending college. See *Science and Engineering Indicators 1996* (Washington, D.C.: National Science Foundation, NSB-96-21, 1996), 7–17. Those percentages are certainly larger today.

12. "Internet Rationing Hits Higher Ed," *The Chronicle of Higher Education*, 4 October 1996, A23.

13. See the "World Lecture Hall" at the University of Texas, available online at http://www.utexas.edu/world/lecture/index.html; also see the University of Houston's "Archive.edu" online at http://www.coe.uh.edu/archive/.

14. See the list of online economics courses at http://www.utexas.edu/world/lecture/eco/. This Microeconomics course from the University of Delaware can be found online at http://medusa.be.udel.edu/WWW_Sites/oo_Micro.html.

15. Beginning in 1988, Rensselaer Polytechnic Institute (RPI) redesigned its introductory undergraduate courses in mathematics, physics, chemistry, biology, and engineering to emphasize cooperative group learning with extensive use of media and computers. Large lectures and traditional laboratories have largely been replaced by small-group "studio" sessions and computer-based data acquisition and analysis. RPI's studio courses require fewer contact hours and have lower costs than did the traditional courses they replaced. Moreover, "evaluations are demonstrating that students learn the material better and faster." See Jack M. Wilson, "Reengineering the Undergraduate Curriculum," in *The Learning Revolution*, 107–128.

16. Some comparisons among media for distance learning can be found in Lynnette R. Porter, *Creating the Virtual Classroom: Distance Learning with the Internet* (New York: John Wiley & Sons, 1997).

17. Prospectus, UOL Publishing, Inc., 26 November 1996, 31.

18. " '[There] is evidence that there's money to be made in this business,' says Jim Mingle, executive director of the State Higher Education Executive Officers." See "Ivy League Eyes Distance Learning," *The Chronicle of Higher Education*, 20 June 1997.

19. As Terry Anderson writes in "Alternative Media for Education Delivery" (http://www.atl.ualberta.ca/papers/alt_media.html), ". . . research over the past seventy years has generally concluded that there are no significant differences between learning delivered face-to-face and that delivered by alternative media."

20. Professor Richard Clark of the University of Southern California concluded his 1983 review article with a strong affirmation of this point: ". . . media are mere vehicles that deliver instruction, but do not influence student achievement any more than the truck that delivers our groceries causes changes in our nutrition." R. E. Clark, "Reconsidering Research on Learning from Media," *Review of Educational Research* 53, no. 4 (1983): 445. See also Thomas L. Russell, "The 'No Significant Difference' Phenomenon as reported in 248 Research Reports, Summaries, and Papers" (4th ed.), available online at http://tenb.mta.ca/phenom/nsd.doc.

21. John Seely Brown and Paul Duguid, "Universities in the Digital Age," *Change*, July/August 1996, 11–19.

22. Higher-speed Internet access via Digital Subscriber Lines (xDSL) and cable modems is now in the early stages of deployment in the telephone and cable networks, respectively. How quickly it will become available and affordable for distance learning depends on a variety of technical, market, and regulatory developments; but the trends seem promising. Paul Kagan Associates, a firm that tracks media-market developments, forecasts that five percent of home Internet subscribers will have high-speed access within ten years. See "Kagan Forecasts $46B in Interactive Revenue by 2007," *Cowles/Simba Media Daily*, 30 July 1997.

23. An April 1997 survey for *Business Week* found that twenty-nine percent of respondents aged eighteen to twenty-four were Internet users—twice the percentage reported in 1996. An additional twelve percent used online services such as America Online or CompuServe. Moreover, a recent *Sports Illustrated* survey reported that about half of the nine-to-thirteen-year-olds polled had used online services or the Internet. "*Business Week*/Harris Poll: A Census in Cyberspace," *Business Week*, 5 May 1997; "What Kids Do On-Line," *USA Today*, 23 June 1997.

24. See the Open University online at http://cszx.open.ac.uk/.

25. Quoted from the Open University's home page at http://cszx.open.ac.uk/zx/HomePage.html.

26. See CSU's MSQA On-Line at http://www.csudh.edu/msqa/msqahome.htm, and CSU–Sonoma State's Composite B.A. Degree Program in Liberal Studies online at http://www.sonoma.edu/exed/lsdcp/ls2.html.

27. CSU Commission on the Extended University, "Annual Report 1995" (Long Beach, Calif.: California State University, 1996), 11.

28. See the CSU–Long Beach Certified Specialist in Planned Giving Program online at http://www.uol.com/csulb.

29. Elaine Woo, "Virtual Colleges," *Los Angeles Times Campus and Career Guide*, 20 July 1997, 2.

30. See the Home Education Network at http://www.then.com/.

31. Cited in Woo, "Virtual Colleges." See UC–Berkeley Extension online at http://www-cmil.unex.berkeley.edu/online/.

32. "UOL Publishing and UC–Berkeley Extension Sign Agreement to Launch Online Education Program," News Release, 19 May 1997; available online at http://www.uol.com/.

33. Lisa Gubernick and Ashlea Ebeling, "I Got My Degree Through E-mail," *Forbes*, 16 June 1997, 84–86. See the Fuqua School of Business online at http://www.fuqua.duke.edu/programs/gemba/index.htm.

34. See Park College online at http://www.park.edu/dist/course.html.

35. See the VCU/MCV Executive Masters Program in Health Administration online at http://www.vcu.edu/mdcweb/haeweb/.

36. Western Governors' Association, press release, 1 December 1995. (See the Western Governors' University online at http://www.west.gov.org/. Governor Pete Wilson of California declined to join the Western Governors' University consortium and subsequently established a separate California Virtual University Design Team (Governor's Office, press release, 4 April 1997).

37. Michael O. Leavitt, "The Western Governors' University: A Learning Enterprise for the CyberCentury," quoted at http://www.west.gov.org/smart/vu/faq.htm; reprinted in *The Learning Revolution*, 180–94. Much of the detailed planning that describes the structure, financing, and operation of the Western Governors' University is available online at http://www.west.gov.org/smart/vu/vu.htm.

38. Quoted online at http://www.international.edu/iu/mission.html.

39. Quoted online at http://www.athena.edu/overview.html.

40. See the League for Innovation in the Community Colleges online at http://www.league.org/itpartnr.html.

41. See the online list of the University of Nottingham's Web-based courses at http://www.vsms.nottingham.ac.uk/vsms/catalog.html.

42. Quoted from IBM press release, 10 October 1996. See the IBM Global Campus online at http://www.hied.ibm.com/igc/.

43. See UOL Publishing, Inc., online at http://www.uol.com.

44. See the CSU–Long Beach Certified Specialist in Planned Giving Program online at http://www.uol.com/csulb.

45. See the Georgetown University School of Business online course at http://www. uol.com/georgetown/.

46. See the GMU program online at http://www.pubs.gmu.edu/catalog/gradbusi.html.

47. The Bureau of the Census, Department of Commerce, estimates a 1995 total of $52 billion for corporate training and education. Although the available disaggre-gated data are not very precise, as much as $10 billion of corporate training is now delivered via PC software, CD-ROM, videotape, videodisk, client-server comput-er systems, Internet, and Intranets. The Gartner Group projects that the demand for technology-based training will rise ten percent a year for the next two years. Quality Dynamics, Inc., predicts that by the year 2000, "half of all corporate train-ing will be delivered via technology." Both quoted in *Information Week*, 4 November 1996, 32.

48. See the Microsoft Online Institute at http://moli.microsoft.com/.

49. See Oracle at http://ola.us.oracle.com/.

50. R. Poulin and J. Witherspoon discuss Novell Education (http://education. novell.com/) in "Best Practices in Implementation of Advanced Educational Technologies" (Boulder, Colo: Western Interstate Commission for Higher Education, April 1996).

51. See Autodesk's Virtual Campus at http://www.vcampus/com.

52. See Dun & Bradstreet Information Services online at http://www.uol.com/dbis/.

53. See the University of Phoenix online at http://www.uophx.edu; see Apollo Group, Inc., online at http://www.apollogrp.com.

54. Ethan Bronner, "University for Working Adults Shatters Mold, *New York Times*, 15 October 1997, A1.

55. The figure of twenty-six hundred online students is reported in "For-Profit U.," available online at http://www.forbes.com/forbes/97/0616/5912084a.htm. Degrees offered by the University of Phoenix for online study are: B.S. in Business, M.B.A., M.A. in Organizational Management, and M.S. in Computer Information Systems. See http://www.uophx.edu/online.

56. Poulin and Witherspoon, "Best Practices in Implementation of Advanced Educational Technologies."

57. Cost studies have been commissioned by the League For Innovation in the Community Colleges and the Western Governors' University, among others, but their results are not yet publicly available.

58. Gubernick and Ebeling, "I Got My Degree Through E-mail." The higher cost of Internet over conventional courses at these campuses (Duke University, University of Maine, University of Phoenix) probably reflects institutional estimates of stu-dent demand elasticity rather than any underlying cost structure.

59. William F. Massey, "Life on the Wired Campus: How Information Technology Will Shape Institutional Futures," in *The Learning Revolution*, 195–210. For an estimate of faculty time and resulting cost savings from the RPI studio courses, see William F. Massy and Robert Zemsky, *Using Information Technology to Enhance Academic Productivity* (Washington, D.C.: EDUCOM, 1995).

60. See, for example, Terry O'Banion, "Transforming the Community College from a Teaching to a Learning Institution," in *The Learning Revolution*, 138–53.

61. Federal Communications Commission, *Universal Service Report & Order*, FCC 97-57, Section 10, 7 May 1997.

62. All of the major academic publishers are jockeying for roles as creators and distributors of Internet-based courseware. It is also likely that non-publishing firms such as AT&T, EDS, Sylvan Learning Systems, Andersen Consulting, Bellcore/SAIC and others, including many outside the U.S., will enter the Internet education and training market.

63. Clara Lovett, President of Northern Arizona University, quoted in Leavitt, "The Western Governors' University."

64. Others may be more willing to forecast a specific date by which higher education will have profoundly changed. For example, Peter Schwartz, the prominent futurist, and Peter Leyden present a scenario in which information technology first spurs innovation and reform in U.S. elementary and secondary schools "starting in earnest in 2000." The scenario continues:

> Higher education, though slightly less in need of an overhaul, catches the spirit of radical reform. . . . The vigorous adoption of networking technologies benefits undergraduate and graduate students even more than K–12 kids. In 2001, Project Gutenberg completes its task of putting ten thousand books online. Many of the world's leading universities begin carving off areas of expertise and assuming responsibility for the digitalization of all the literature in that field. Around 2010, all new books come out in electronic form. . . .

Peter Schwartz and Peter Leyden, "The Long Boom: A History of the Future, 1980–2020," *Wired*, July 1997, 169–70.

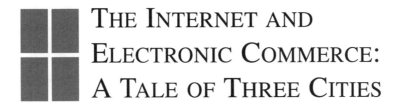

THE INTERNET AND ELECTRONIC COMMERCE: A TALE OF THREE CITIES

Elliot Maxwell

Deputy Chief, Office of Plans and Policy
Federal Communications Commission

As the French Internet Interministerial Commission has noted, the Internet is rapidly evolving from "a closed world of specialists and experts to a common and commercial universe open to the general public."[1] Over the last several years, the number of Internet users, as well as the range of commercial applications for which the Internet is being used, have grown tremendously. In response to the rapid growth of Internet-based global electronic commerce, which is projected to quickly reach multibillion dollar levels,[2] governments around the world are struggling to develop policy frameworks to accommodate this new reality.

In 1997, the European Commission and the governments of the United States and Japan conducted policy reviews of Internet commerce. In April, Japan's Ministry of International Trade and Industry released a draft policy paper, "Towards the Age of the Digital Economy—For Rapid Growth in the Japanese Economy in the Twenty-First Century" (hereinafter "Digital Economy"), which proposed that increased investment in information technology could reinvigorate, and help transform, the Japanese economy.[3] In the same month, the European Commission issued "A European Initiative in Electronic

The opinions and conclusions of this paper are those of the author and do not necessarily reflect the views of the Federal Communications Commission (FCC), any of its Commissioners or staff members, or any other entities or employees of the U.S. government.

Commerce" (hereinafter "Initiative"), aimed at encouraging "the vigorous growth of electronic commerce in Europe" and thus increasing "Europe's competitiveness in global markets."[4] In July, U.S. President Bill Clinton issued "Framework for Global Electronic Commerce" (hereinafter "Framework"), designed to "permit consumers, workers, and entrepreneurs to develop the full potential of global economic commerce."[5]

As important first policy statements from the leading industrialized countries about the Internet and electronic commerce, these three documents are providing a foundation for international negotiations over electronic commerce policy. Overall they voice agreement on many key points.[6] They all take a positive view of Internet development, stressing the societal benefits of its growth and highlighting the prospects for, and the potential gains from, electronic commerce; they all view the Internet as a global institution, rather than a national or regional one; and they all acknowledge that the Internet raises important new issues that require global resolution.

But profound differences—often only hinted at in the policy statements themselves—exist among the U.S., Japanese, and European approaches to electronic commerce, differences that are likely to become more important as governments move from the enunciation of broad policy principles towards the implementation of concrete policies. As Peter Drucker has noted, "All great plans eventually degenerate into real work."[7]

Such differences should come as no surprise, of course; disparities in international policy commonly arise due to different legal regimes, different customs, and different policy approaches to the questions that every country must address. But the differences will only be exacerbated if governments fall back on traditional policy frameworks while the rate of technological change, and the rate at which new policy issues emerge, outpace the policy-making process.

All three policy papers resonate with an optimism about the future that is helping to animate the necessary policy dialogue. But as with most discussions about new technologies, early optimism must be tempered with more considered pragmatism. Toward that end, this chapter bypasses the large and important areas of agreement among the three policy statements to focus on some of the potential potholes in the road to the bright future that the documents foresee: national differences in ideas about the role of government in electronic commerce and the nature of government itself; and public-policy problems of jurisdiction, taxes and duties, content regulation, privacy, and standards development. By highlighting these differences, I hope to help identify topics where greater efforts will be required to achieve global understanding.

THE ROLE OF GOVERNMENT IN
ELECTRONIC COMMERCE

All three policy documents urge a limited role for government in electronic commerce. As the U.S. "Framework" notes,

> Governments can have a profound effect on the growth of commerce on the Internet. By their actions, they can facilitate electronic trade or inhibit it. Knowing when to act and—at least as important—when not to act, will be crucial to the development of electronic commerce.

The U.S. "Framework" attempts to define the respective roles of government and the private sector by enunciating several overriding principles:

- The private sector should lead.

- Governments should avoid undue restrictions on electronic commerce.

- Where governmental involvement is needed, its aim should be to support and enforce a predictable, minimalist, consistent, and simple legal environment for commerce.

In a similar vein, the European "Initiative" notes four principles designed to "provide the [European] Union with an adaptable and appropriate framework for legislation":

- No regulation for regulation's sake.

- Any regulation must be based on all Single Market freedoms.

- Any regulation must take account of business realities.

- Any regulation must meet general interest objectives effectively and efficiently.

The Japanese "Digital Economy" report, in turn, stresses that problems relating to electronic commerce should be solved "by technological means, as well as competition in the marketplace or through creation
of new independent business practices in the private sector," not by
"immediately adopting regulations." It continues: "If regulations should
become unavoidable, they should be kept at a minimum taking into con-
sideration the interest to be protected by the law and harmonization with
traditional solutions to similar issues."

This orientation toward private-sector leadership in the development of electronic commerce policy, and reliance on technical or market-oriented solutions involving minimal governmental intervention has
received broad acceptance from political and industry figures. But it is
still early in the political process, and the policy battles about electronic commerce are likely to be fought on far narrower grounds.

While all three policy statements suggest a "hands-off" approach to
electronic commerce, it is unclear whether they represent a firm enough
consensus to constrain their respective governments from attempting to
exercise control over the Internet and electronic commerce. This is particularly true given the economic importance that both the European
and Japanese governments attach to development of a successful
Internet policy. Both the Japanese and European papers express a sense
of urgency that, because the United States is well in the lead in Internet
and electronic commerce development, other nations must move quickly to catch up or suffer defeat in global markets.

In response, the European "Initiative" calls for action to ensure that
electronic commerce jobs are "created and maintained in the European
Single Market." It outlines a "comprehensive set of actions" aimed at
building on what are deemed Europe's inherent strengths in the Internet
world, so that Europe can become the "heartland of electronic commerce." These actions include providing high-bandwidth infrastructure
and giving "special importance in a number of R&D programmes to
electronic commerce." In order to promote a "favourable business environment," the European paper's agenda includes training, information,
and demonstration projects as well as special actions aimed at small-
and medium-sized enterprises. The European paper also contemplates
regulatory responses addressed, in appropriate cases, "at every step of
the business activity, from the establishment of business, to the promotion and provision of electronic commerce activities, through conclu-

sion of contracts, to the making of electronic payments." What it does not make clear are the relative roles of public and private players in these new initiatives, nor does it discuss the openness of the European processes and programs to non-Europeans—a potential source of conflict with other countries.

Although the Japanese paper provides a far less-detailed road map for government action, its goals are at least as ambitious. It seeks the "reconversion of the industrial structure of the past" and a "reformation in the entire economic structure of Japan."

The emphasis on regional competition evident in these two papers is disturbing, because electronic commerce should be an "engine for economic growth"[8]—as the U.S.–European Union (EU) joint statement on electronic commerce characterized it—not a battleground between countries. Government policies should facilitate global electronic commerce, rather than being judged by whether they successfully advance the interests of any one region. A mercantilist orientation aimed at favoring any one entity over another is likely to slow the development of global agreements and thus slow the growth of electronic commerce for all.

THE NATURE OF GOVERNMENT

Also undermining agreement among the United States, Europe, and Japan are different beliefs about the nature of government and the extent of its responsibilities. The history of the United States reveals a thread of political skepticism that can be traced back to the country's founders: a distrust of the power of government and a belief that its role should be checked. When new technologies come on the scene, that skepticism supports—as the U.S. "Framework" endorses—a moratorium on governmental action until the market matures or has the opportunity to evolve market-based solutions to potential problems. There is much to commend in a tradition that, when confronted by the new, allocates experimental time and space for policy development.[9]

Neither European nor Japanese thought is characterized by the same skepticism about government. In particular, the European response, when confronted by issues raised by new technologies, seems more likely to be an attempt to anticipate, study, and forestall all possible outcomes thought to undermine the public interest. Advocates of a minimalist role for government therefore were not surprised by European Commissioner Martin Bangemann's call for an "international charter for global communications" and a new "single European regulatory authority for communications and media services" in a speech to the Telecom Interactive '97 Conference in Geneva.[10] Since the end of World War II in particular, the Japanese government has played a powerful role in the operation of the Japanese economy, a role that has enjoyed strong public support given its perceived contribution to Japan's successful rise as a world economic superpower. Yet Japan's agonizingly slow recovery from the collapse of the "bubble economy," combined with what appears to be an increasing Japanese consensus about the need for deregulation throughout Japanese society, suggests that the role of government in Internet regulation will be the subject of robust internal debate.

A second crucial set of questions relates to the circumstances under which governments *should* exercise power. Is there a minimal level of regulation required to enable electronic commerce? If so, what is it? If the private sector is to lead, and if governments are to defer to private decision making, what decision-making processes and dispute resolution procedures must private-sector actors put in place? How open and robust must they be? Will government pledges to respect private-sector decisions be considered binding even when those decisions are politically unsatisfactory to governmental decision makers? Under what circumstances will administrations act affirmatively to provide legitimacy to private-sector decision making? Given the unprecedented characteristics of the Internet—its global nature, its potential to "route around" governmental controls (just as it was designed to route around failures in its physical infrastructure), and its capacity to link people and information—new forms of decision making are likely to be required.

JURISDICTION

The question of the extent of governmental involvement or control may, in fact, be less important than the question of *which* government has control. Many of the most difficult questions surrounding electronic commerce are those of jurisdiction—who has the power to decide which issue. Yet the three policy papers provide little guidance in this area.

The questions are fundamental. Can any single government assert control over a specific action involving the Internet? If so, for any given action, which government should that be? And whose rules should it apply—its own, the rules of other governments, or a whole new set of rules reflecting the Internet's challenges to national sovereignty? How far will today's calls for devolution of policy making be taken when applied to an inherently global institution? In the United States, what decisions will be made at the national level, as opposed to that of states or counties or cities? In the European Union, what decisions will, by the principle of subsidiarity, be taken at the local or national as opposed to the European level? In Japan, will power continue to be exercised from imperial Tokyo or will it devolve to other levels of government? And how will the potential fragmentation of policy affect the development of electronic commerce? The very global nature of the Internet makes these jurisdictional issues both central and confounding.

The United States has begun to face these issues in cases such as those involving Internet gambling. Can a court in state A, where electronic gambling is illegal, stop a company headquartered in state B, where electronic gambling is legal, from offering it to state A's citizens (or, potentially, to anyone)? How does one determine where the legal or illegal action takes place—in state A, at the site of the computer used to access the Internet? in state B, the physical address of the electronic gambling company? in state C, location of the server that hosts the gambling site? or in any state at all that houses a router through which the communications pass on the Internet?[11]

U.S. courts have found no consistent answer. One federal court has suggested that Missouri may not be able to apply its consumer protection laws to an Internet gambling service operated out of a server located on a Native American reservation, because the states have no authority over gambling "on Indian lands."[12] But a state court in Minnesota, taking a drastically different approach, has held that Minnesota can apply its own consumer protection laws to a Nevada web site advertising Internet gambling, on the grounds that the site is accessible to Minnesota viewers (as it is to viewers throughout the world).[13]

Nor is gambling the only arena in which jurisdictional questions will arise. The areas of securities regulation, banking, intellectual property, data privacy, regulation of professional services, consumer protection, and access to allegedly harmful material are only a few areas posing obvious jurisdictional questions. When a person purchases an item via the World Wide Web, what antifraud, contract, and usury rules should apply? What country's laws should govern Internet content that arguably is defamatory, or sexually explicit, or promotes race hatred? Hate speech and racist literature are, after all, protected in the United States, but criminal under the laws of countries such as Germany and Canada. And the uncertainties surrounding jurisdiction are compounded by the heightened possibility of anonymity offered by the Internet, which provides both needed protection to the vulnerable and impenetrable disguises for wrongdoers. Successful resolution of the jurisdictional issues—whether posed between states within the United States, or between countries in the European Union, or between countries that do not recognize each other or have chosen not to participate in international agreements concerning particular activities—is likely to be necessary to provide the stable and minimalist legal environment that all three papers argue is a prerequisite for the successful growth of electronic commerce. Given the traditional reluctance of countries to cede authority to any other entities, be they other governments or multilateral organizations, this promises to be an issue requiring intense and imaginative efforts.

Another crucial jurisdictional issue relates to governance of the Internet itself. Much of the Internet's early, precommercial development was funded and overseen by the U.S. government. This early governmental involvement has left the U.S. government with some residual authority over the operation of the Internet. Claims for a broadening or narrowing of this authority have been heard, for example, in the sometimes shrill debate over domain names—the mnemonic devices that, when associated with numerical addresses, facilitate access to Internet resources.

Today, the domain-name system is in transition due to the desire for more competition in its operation as well as the globalization of the Internet and the widely held belief that the private sector should play the lead role in its governance. When the debate over the future shape of the domain-name system began, many people advocated a hands-off policy by government, arguing that the "Internet community" should make the decisions about this policy issue and presumably others.[14]

Yet the processes for such self-governance are not yet obvious. Who is the "Internet community"? How will it make decisions? How does one participate in such a decision-making process? What roles should be played by governments or multilateral organizations in those processes? As the Internet evolves, the issues of how decisions will be made, and by whom, will continue to emerge. New relationships will need to be proposed between governments (traditionally the grantors of authority) and newly empowered private-sector decision makers. New models for private-sector decision making must be created, with processes sufficiently fair and robust that the decisions they yield will be viewed as legitimate by the "Internet community"—which, more and more, appears to be synonymous with us all.

TAXES AND DUTIES

Internet-based electronic commerce has the potential to create a burgeoning new revenue stream for governments hard pressed for funds. As students of American history know, some answers to the question of who has a right to tax and what is subject to taxation can lead to revolutionary action. The Internet raises these questions to new heights by making national borders transparent and by providing a potential cloak for the identities and locations of parties to commercial transactions.

The U.S. "Framework" recommends that the Internet be treated as a tariff-free environment whenever it is used to deliver products or services, with a ban on new Internet taxes. The United States has already seen state and local attempts to raise revenues by taxing many Internet-related activities. The U.S. Treasury Department has issued a policy paper aimed at developing a federal policy framework for taxation,[15] and several congressional initiatives for freezing new state and local Internet taxes have been proposed.[16]

The potential of electronic commerce to yield new tax revenue is as tempting to European and Japanese national and local authorities as it is to state and local governments in the United States. Proposals for Internet taxes at the national level have already arisen in Europe, only to be stopped at the level of the European Union, and disputes have arisen at the national level over the application of value-added taxes to electronic commerce. Given Europe's greater reliance on indirect taxes, it is likely that conflicts over how to deal with Internet taxes will be at least as contentious there as in the United States. The European "Initiative" raises the issue of taxation but doesn't resolve it; it calls for legal certainty so that "tax obligations are clear, transparent, and predictable," as well as for tax neutrality between electronic commerce and more traditional commerce while "preventing undue revenue loss."

The Japanese "Digital Economy" report reflects similar concerns about the application of value-added taxes, given the uncertain location of buyers and sellers. It is striking that there is, as of the end of 1997, no policy statement on Internet taxation from Japan's powerful Ministry of Finance.

The fact that questions of taxation and duties have been the focus of extended international dialogue is promising. Work in the Organization for Economic Cooperation and Development (OECD) to avoid "double taxation" and promote bilateral and multilateral consultations have brought the major industrialized nations closer together.[17] Much work, however, remains to be done to achieve the certainty that the three policy papers prescribe.

CONTENT REGULATION

It has often been noted that the information superhighway runs through some very bad neighborhoods. Real tensions exist between those who appreciate the heightened access to information made possible by the Internet and those who desire to prevent the dissemination of material alleged to be harmful, particularly to classes of users (such as children) who are thought to be most vulnerable. All of the policy papers attempt, in one way or another, to deal with these tensions. Similarly, all of the policy papers recognize that there may well be activities conducted on the Internet that would constitute crimes in one or another jurisdiction.[18]

The U.S. "Framework" argues for the free flow of information, and against censorship of the Internet; users should be empowered to control the content they encounter with the assistance of techniques such as rating and filtering systems, combined with industry self-regulation. There is a growing debate in the U.S. over rating and filtering systems. Supporters argue that such systems improve the control that parents, for instance, have over the exposure of their children to harmful material;

opponents see the same systems as potential tools for oppressive governments.[19] The "Framework" recognizes that issues are likely to arise internationally over government restrictions on Internet content including, for example, restrictions on pornographic and seditious material, quotas for content based on national origin, enforcement of differing national policies on advertising, and the protection of consumers from fraudulent information.

The Japanese "Digital Economy" statement envisions shared responsibility among governments, carriers, content providers, and users. The report notes that there are "illegal and harmful contents" on the Internet, including "slander and libel, racial discrimination and obscenity," "violent material," and "unlawful information on drugs." It suggests, as does the "Framework," that such content can be addressed through "voluntary efforts by providers of information and network providers, as well as the technology of these providers." The Japanese paper advocates user-controlled refusal and selection mechanisms rather than governmental control.

In 1996 the European Commission issued a communication on "Illegal and Harmful Content on the Internet,"[20] and in 1997 followed up with an "Action Plan"[21] on the same topic. Like both the U.S. "Framework" and the Japanese report on the "Digital Economy," the European "Initiative" proposes filtering and rating software as well as public education as the principal means of dealing with "harmful" (adult or offensive) content. But it goes far beyond the American or Japanese efforts—and reflects present European law and regulation— by identifying a wide range of illegal content that might be carried on the Internet. The action plan assumes the need for governments to address:

- national security (instructions on bomb making, illegal drug production, terrorist activities)

- protection of minors (abusive forms of marketing, violence, pornography)

- protection of human dignity (incitement to racial hatred or racial discrimination)

- economic security (fraud, instructions on pirating credit cards)

- information security (malicious hacking)

- protection of privacy (unauthorized communication of personal data, electronic harassment)
- protection of reputation (libel, unlawful comparative advertising)
- intellectual property (unauthorized distribution of copyrighted works)

To control this wide range of materials the European Commission contemplates an equally wide range of control mechanisms. It supports a "fully functioning system of self-regulation" including industry codes of conduct to restrict circulation of such material, as well as self-regulation on the part of Internet Service Providers (ISPs). The EU anticipates its own funding of research and development of filtering mechanisms, a course that the U.S. government has sought to avoid. Rules already in effect have moved discussions from the policy papers to the courts, where battles are being fought over such issues as rules in France that require sites to use the national language, or conflicts between rules in Germany that prohibit (in Germany) content such as displays of Nazi insignia or of hate speech and rules in other countries (such as the U.S.) which do not criminalize such content—demonstrating once again the importance of jurisdictional issues.

Some content providers are likely to hesitate before engaging in electronic commerce on the Internet due to a lack of certainty about legal liability resulting from differing legal regimes. And some online service providers are likely to be caught up in struggles between countries such as Germany, which may hold them liable for content posted by others, and countries that, at least in some contexts, immunize them from such liability.[22]

In the long run, it may well be that the impact of debates over content regulation will not be felt most severely in the area of "adult content," the area of seemingly greatest public concern—and profitability—in the United States. Because of differing legal and regulatory traditions, the effect may be greater in other commercial arenas such as advertising, promotion, and provision of professional services protected to some extent in the United States by the First Amendment but subject to more intense governmental scrutiny in other countries.

PRIVACY

For the last quarter century, Americans have identified privacy protection as an important public policy issue. The same technologies that have contributed to the development of the Internet have made the gathering and manipulation of data, including personal data, easy and cheap; in fact, such data is now regarded as "fuel" for electronic commerce.[23]

Within the U.S. government the Federal Trade Commission (FTC) has played the lead role regarding privacy and commerce. The FTC has conducted investigations and hearings about online privacy that have examined industry self-regulatory proposals, as well as proposals for governmental action.[24] The FTC's recent actions are consistent with the support provided by the U.S. "Framework" for private-sector efforts "to implement meaningful, consumer friendly, self-regulatory privacy regimes," and with its understanding that many privacy issues are amenable to technical solutions allowing consumers to make their own choices regarding disclosure of non-public information. The U.S. "Framework" does recognize that certain groups, such as children, require different treatment, given their inability to understand privacy notices or provide informed consent for disclosure of personal non-public information.

The Japanese, while having a less well-developed body of privacy law, have traditionally taken a sector-by-sector approach to privacy similar to that of the United States. The "Digital Economy" approach to privacy continues this trend, relying on voluntary, industry-specific guidelines, as well as on increased privacy options for consumers, bolstered by consumer-education campaigns to heighten awareness of the issue.

In contrast, the EC has promulgated a broad directive on the protection of personal data.[25] The European "Initiative" suggests that the privacy directive may be supplemented by specific measures to address privacy in the context of electronic commerce. The privacy directive has already been identified as a possible source of conflict between the United States and Europe; the directive bars the transfer of personal data to countries that—in the Commission's view—don't extend adequate privacy protection to EU citizens. Whether the sector-by-sector U.S. and Japanese approaches will meet the EU's standard is not yet clear, although this topic has been the subject of numerous discussions among the parties. The potential extraterritorial effect of the European privacy directive has been of particular concern.

The privacy arena also illustrates another potential conflict. When discussing self-regulation, U.S. commentators often mean just that— private groups making decisions that limit their behaviors, bound only by broad laws of general application, not specific laws targeted to the area in which self-regulation is to take place. Such self-regulation may take place under watchful governmental eyes or with the implied threat of governmental action. The European vision of self-regulation, in contrast, assumes that the private, self-regulatory actions will take place within a framework set by the government, and will derive their authority from that of the government. Implementation of international agreements based on self-regulation will surely be difficult if the same words have significantly different meanings to the parties involved.

STANDARDS AND INTEROPERABILITY

While the Internet may not have been "born global" in the words of the European "Initiative," it became so in its formative years. Its success has been based on the massive voluntary adoption of the open Internet Protocol, which allows seamless communications among disparate networks and equipment.

The U.S. "Framework" strongly endorses the use of the "marketplace, not governments" to determine technical standards and other mechanisms for interoperability. It urges "industry driven multilateral fora" to consider standards in such areas as "electronic payments, . . . security (confidentiality, authentication, data integrity, access control, non-repudiation), and security services infrastructure (e.g., public key certificate authorities)." The pace of events may be outrunning U.S. policymakers' desire to use such fora; by the close of 1997, thirty-nine U.S. states had legislated in the area of digital signatures, potentially fragmenting the market and creating barriers to global solutions.

While recognizing the importance of industry participation, European and Japanese governments have traditionally played a more active role in standards developments. To counter the effects of disparate actions at the national level (there were, as of the end of 1997, four separate nationally based digital signature standards in Europe) the European Commission plans to launch specific actions on standardization projects for electronic commerce. It advocates a European standardization initiative for electronic commerce, identifying technical barriers and proposing concrete steps to remove them.

The Japanese "Digital Economy" report also recognizes the need for governmental action—"the flexible application of the process of public standardization"—noting that market-based standards may possibly impede the workings of the marketplace. The Japanese document stresses the importance of assuring the openness of different types of interfaces, raising the contentious issue of compulsory licensing.

It is in this developing area of standards that the harmony exemplified in the adoption of the Internet Protocol is most likely to break down. Multinational corporations engaged in furious struggles with each other will often seek, and many times find, nations willing to act as their national champions. And governmental processes, more recently dominated in the United States by lawyers, will have to struggle to identify and resolve technical issues that may have profound impacts on the development of electronic commerce.

CONCLUSION

These issues of the regulation of electronic commerce do not exhaust the areas of possible disagreement. Differing approaches to intellectual-property questions such as the greater protection offered by Europeans to database creators have already created such controversy within the U.S. research community that agreements were blocked at the last World Intellectual Property Organization meeting.[26] Differing applications of existing regulations to new Internet-based services (such as Internet telephony, which has been prohibited by Portugal and Hungary, but found insufficiently established to be regulated as telephony by the European Commission)[27] may slow the global availability of new services to consumers. Different views as to the desirability of providing "strong" encryption to every citizen and the impact of such availability on law-enforcement and intelligence activities may reduce the security available for commercial transactions on the Internet[28] and slow its adoption as a mass-market vehicle to reach consumers.

The coming months will undoubtedly bring important bilateral and multilateral negotiations aimed at developing the global understandings anticipated by the three policy papers. The U.S. "Framework" identified many of the fora in which agreements can be struck. And there are important models for success, such as the World Trade Organization agreements opening up telecommunications markets around the globe.

But beyond the intra- and intergovernmental negotiations will be an even broader policy discussion conducted on the Internet. The Internet will continue to serve as an electronic Hyde Park Corner, allowing every proposal or initiative in cities, states, countries, and bilateral and multilateral fora around the world to be identified, analyzed, and compared. The "Internet community" will be able to watch policy experiments of every type and see their impact on the development of electronic commerce.

And the impact will be visible. The inherent mobility of electronic commerce and the Web sites that make up such an important part of its infrastructure mean that entrepreneurs will gravitate to the most favorable legal environment. Countries will be vying—often with negative results as in the case of data havens and money (or cybercash) laundering—for the legal, if not the physical, presence of significant electronic commerce providers.

Policymakers should give themselves the time to learn from these experiments. We should take the opportunity to utilize the Internet's remarkable capacity for allowing hundreds, even thousands of people to collaborate in developing improved policies and policy-making processes. The more good ideas that we extract, the more that we learn about the distinctive qualities of the Internet, and the more we are prepared to both imaginatively apply existing policies or develop new ones suited to this new institution, the more likely it is that the optimistic visions of these three policy papers can be realized and the vast positive potential of the Internet made available to all the peoples of the world.

ENDNOTES

I am indebted to many people who have examined the emerging literature on electronic commerce. I would like to specifically note the works of Patrick Vittet-Philippe of Directorate-General XIII of the European Commission; Emily M. Murase, of the Institute for Communication Research of Stanford University; and the staff of the GIIC Policy Task Force comparing the policy papers on electronic commerce of the United States, the European Union, and Japan's Ministry of International Trade and Industry.²⁹ Jonathan Weinburg has provided helpful insight on a wide variety of issues, and Greg Guy has helped find the sometimes elusive, sometimes plentiful cites/sites on the World Wide Web. Any errors herein are, however, all my own.

1. The French Interministerial Commission, *Electronic Commerce: A New Factor for Consumers, Companies, Citizens and Government.* Available online at http://www.telecom.gouv.fr/francais/activ/techno/florentzsom.htm.

2. Christopher Anderson, "In Search of the Perfect Market—A Survey of Electronic Commerce," *The Economist*, 10 May 1997, 56+; and Forrester Research, quoted in Edward R. Berryman, "Web Commerce: Be Prepared," *New York Times*, 12 October 1997, 2.

3. "Towards the Age of the Digital Economy—For Rapid Growth in the Japanese Economy in the Twenty-First Century" is available online at http://www.glocom.ac.jp/news/MITI-doc.html.

4. The "European Initiative in Electronic Commerce" is available online at http://www.ispo.cec.be/ecommerce/initial.html.

5. The United States' "Framework for Global Electronic Commerce" is available online at http://www.whitehouse.gov/WH/New/Commerce/.

6. Patrick Vittet-Philippe estimated that the U.S. and EU papers overlapped "by roughly 80 percent." Vittet-Philippe, "A Note for the File, U.S. Policies in Electronic Commerce: A Comparative Analysis of the 'Magaziner Paper,' ('A Framework for Global Electronic Commerce')," 3 July 1997.

7. This and other quotes, works, and papers can be found online at Digital Drucker, http://www.dgsys.com/~tristan/technodrucker.html.

8. The "United States and European Joint Statement on E-Commerce" is available at http://www.state.gov/www/regions/eur/eu/971205_useu_js_electronic.html.

9. To be sure, calls for such a moratorium in the United States are not always so high-minded; they often reflect judgments as to whether one party or another will benefit from government action or inaction.

10. Commissioner Bangemann's speech to the "Telecom Interactive '97 Conference" is available online at http://www.ispo.cec.be/infosoc/promo/speech/geneva.html.

11. See http://www.uslottery.com.

12. *Missouri v Couer D'Alene Tribe*, No. 97-0914-CV-W-6 (WD Mo 29 September 1997).

13. *Minnesota v Granite Gate Resorts*, No. C6-97-89 (Minn Ct App 5 September 1997).

14. For various responses to the International Ad Hoc Committee (IAHC) proposal and the National Telecommunications and Information Administration (NTIA) request for comments, see the Web page of the World Internetworking Alliance (WIA) at http://www.wia.org. More information on the IAHC proposal is available online: For the "Generic Top Level Domain Memorandum of Understanding," see http://www.gtld-mou.org. For the "Request for Comments on the Registration and Administration of Internet Domain Names," see http://www.ntia.doc.gov/ntiahome/domainname/dn5notic.htm.

15. "Selected Tax Policy Implications of Global Electronic Commerce," U.S. Department of Treasury, Office of Tax Policy, November 1996.

16. See http://thomas.loc.gov. for S.442, "Internet Tax Freedom Act," introduced by Senator Ron Wyden on 13 March 1997; and H.R. 1054, "Internet Tax Freedom Act," introduced by Representative Christopher Cox on 13 March 1997.

17. According to "Dismantling the Barriers to Global Electronic Commerce," a paper presented at the Organization for Economic Cooperation and Development (OECD):

> The OECD's Fiscal Affairs Committee (CFA) has set up four study groups to research and investigate how the development of e-commerce affects the current tax systems for direct and indirect taxation, and to consider increased opportunities for tax avoidance and evasion and other tax administration issues. This work reviews the basic concepts of taxation of the OECD Model Tax Convention on Income and Capital as they relate to this new environment, the potential difficulties in applying the OECD Transfer Pricing Guidelines when intra-group transactions are carried out electronically, the implications for VAT concepts of place of supply and issues concerning the identification of taxpayers and the traceability of transactions. Study groups are required to put forward recommendations for internationally consistent solutions to the CFA in January 1998.

This report is available at http://www.oecd.org/dsti/sti/it/ec/prod/DISMANTL.HTM. In addition, see the OECD's "Electronic Commerce: The Challenges to Tax Authorities and Taxpayers," available at http://www.oecd.org/daf/fa/TURKU18.PDF.

18. This recognition has led to meetings between law-enforcement authorities in the developed countries to increase cooperation and prevent the creation of a lawless frontier in the borderless world.

19. See, for example, Amy Harmon, "Rules for Filtering Web Content Cause Dispute," available online at http://www.nytimes.com/library/cyber/week/011998filter.html. Recent announcements by the government of Vietnam banning visits to sites likely to "incite violence," "undermine national unity," or sow hatred," (story available online at http://www.nytimes.com/library/cyber/week/121397vietnam.html), and by the government of China, which seeks to impose criminal punishment for Internet providers and users who spread "harmful information" via the Web (see http://wired.com/news/email/member/politics/story/9423.html.), are likely to buttress the views of those opposed to filtering.

20. The European Commission's "Communication on Illegal and Harmful Content on the Internet" is available at http://www2.echo.lu/legal/en/internet/communic.html.

21. The European Commission's "Action Plan on Promoting Safe Use of the Internet" is available online at http://www2.echo.lu/legal/en/internet/actplan.html.

22. See *Zeran v America Online, Inc.*, 129 F3d 327 (4th Cir. 1997).

23. For further information concerning privacy and the U.S. National Information Infrastructure, see: "Principles for Providing and Using Personal Information," from the Privacy Working Group, Information Policy Committee, Information Infrastructure Task Force, Washington D.C., Final Version, 6 June 1995 (available online at http://www.iitf.nist.gov/ ipc/ipc/ipcpubs/niiprivprin_final.html). Also see "Options for Promoting Privacy on the National Information Infrastructure," Draft for Public Comment, Information Policy Committee, National Information Infrastructure Task Force, April 1997 (available online at http://www.iitf.nist.gov/ipc/privacy.htm).

24. Federal Trade Commission hearings and reports on privacy are available online at http://www.ftc.gov.

25. The "European Privacy Directive" is available online at http://www2.austlii.edu.au/~graham/PLPR_EU_2.html.

26. The press release concerning the WIPO treaties is available online at http://www.wipo.org/eng/diplconf/distrib/press106.htm. The "International Protection of Copyright and Neighborhood Rights" treaty is available online at http://www.wipo.org/eng/general/copyright/wct.htm. Statements by opponents of aspects of the WIPO treaties can be found at the "EFF 'Intellectual Property-WIPO Copyright & Database Protection Proposals' Archive" online at http://www.eff.org/pub/Intellectual_property/NII_copyright_bill/WIPO.

27. "EU Won't Enforce Normal Telephony Rules on the Net," Computergram, 20 January 1998, available online at http://www.computerwire.com/computergram.

28. "France Proposes Key Encryption Law," *Wall Street Journal*, 20 October 1997. See also "EC report on Ensuring Security and Trust in Electronic Communication," available online at http://www.ispo.cec.bei/eif/policy/97503.html.

29. Those works are: Patrick Vittet-Philippe, "Note for the File, Electronic Commerce: Japanese Policies in the Global Context, A Comparison of the Japanese M.I.T.I. Document 'Towards the Age of the Digital Economy' with the Commission Framework Communication and the U.S. 'Magaziner Paper,'" Directorate General XIII, Telecommunications, Information Market and Exploitation of Research, European Commission, Brussels, 16 May 1997; Emily M. Murase, "Electronic Commerce over the Internet: A Comparison of Policy Directions in the U.S., Europe, and Japan, *Institute for Communication Research*, 27 May 1997, 1–24); and GIIC Policy Task Force, "A Comparison of U.S., EU, and MITI Reports on Electronic Commerce," *I-Ways*, second quarter 1997, 41–51 (available online at http://www.gii.org/egi00256.html).

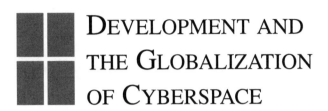

DEVELOPMENT AND THE GLOBALIZATION OF CYBERSPACE

Heather E. Hudson

Director of Telecommunications Management and Policy Program
McLaren School of Business
University of San Francisco

The information revolution provides an invaluable new set of tools for all partners striving to achieve sustainable development. It makes empowerment both meaningful and effective and opens up for developing countries the prospect of leapfrogging over earlier communication technologies to become real participants in the global economy.

Maurice F. Strong
Former Secretary-General, Rio Earth Summit[1]

The history of the Internet—from U.S. defense network to international "virtual college" of scientific and academic researchers to globally expanding World Wide Web—has been one of exponential growth in both number of users and number of hosts connected to the network.[2] While still heavily dominated by the United States in terms of numbers of both users and hosts, the Internet is now widely accessible in all industrialized countries and in major cities of most developing countries. Attempts to extend access within developing countries, however, have been slowed by telecommunications links that are unavailable, unreliable, and/or unaffordable.[3] Now both the telecommunications industry, eager to expand into new markets, and policymakers, convinced that new communications technologies are critical to economic growth, are heeding the call to improve the global "information infrastructure."

This chapter examines issues surrounding access to the Internet in developing countries and the utilization of this powerful information tool for social and economic development. The chapter begins with a discussion of the current national demographics of the Internet. It continues with a survey of international initiatives to benefit developing countries and descriptions of several examples of Internet-related projects in developing countries. The chapter concludes with an analysis of issues of global access to the Internet.

ACCESS TO THE INTERNET: GROWTH AND GAPS

Statistics on Internet access reveal the extent of the discrepancies between high- and low-income nations.[4] (See Table 1.) In 1995, high-income countries had almost 25,000 Internet *users* per 1 million inhabitants, while lower-middle–income countries had fewer than 1,000. The poorest countries had fewer than 20 Internet users per 1 million inhabitants. The extreme scarcity of *hosts* (uniquely reachable connected computers) in poorer, developing countries indicates that access to the Internet there is both difficult and expensive.

Table 1: Internet Access, 1995[5]

Country classification	Internet users/ 1 million inhabitants	Internet hosts/ 1 million inhabitants
High income	24,679.5	10,749.2
Upper-middle income	3,757.5	380.1
Lower-middle income	811.6	73.3
Low income	17.4	1.4

Perhaps the most striking development for both industrialized and developing countries has been the recent exponential growth of the Internet as measured by the number of hosts. Worldwide, the number of hosts grew from fewer than 100,000 in 1989 to more than 16 million by early 1997.[6] Internet *domains* (site addresses, such as those ending in ".com," ".org," ".edu," or a two-digit country code) have also proliferated. The number of Internet domains grew exponentially, from 21,000 in December 1992 to 828,000 in December 1996; growth accelerated sharply in 1995 with increased access to the World Wide Web. And while the United States accounts for the vast majority of Internet sites, this exponential trend was mirrored by many other industrialized countries and also by lower-middle–income and some low-income countries, although the absolute number of sites connected varied from more than 120,000 in major industrialized countries to fewer than 1,000 in some developing countries.[7]

Growth in Internet access has been consistently strong, but it is important to analyze the potential for widespread access to determine whether these growth rates are likely to continue. Two important indicators of this potential are *teledensity*, the availability of infrastructure that connects users to the Internet (measured in telephone lines per 100 inhabitants), and *computer density*, the availability of computer equipment needed for Internet access (measured in computers per 100 inhabitants). (See Table 2.) Industrialized countries possess, on average, more than 50 telephone lines and 20 computers per 100 people. (There is considerable range in computer access even in industrialized countries: While the United States has more than 30 computers per 100 people, Germany, France, and Japan have less than half that number.) Lower-middle–income countries and low-income countries lag far behind in access to both telecommunications and information technologies: Lower-middle–income countries have only about 9 telephone lines and 1 computer per 100 inhabitants; the poorest countries have very limited access to telecommunications and only about 1 computer for every 500 people.

Table 2: Teledensity and Computer Density, 1995[8]

Country classification	Telephone lines/ 100 inhabitants	Personal computers/ 100 inhabitants
High income	53.2	20.5
Upper-middle income	14.5	3.3
Lower-middle income	9.1	1.1
Low income	2.0	0.2

Major disparities also exist within the developing world. Industrializing Asian economies such as the Four Tigers (Hong Kong, South Korea, Singapore, and Taiwan) have invested much more in information and communication technologies than have Latin American countries and the emerging economies of Eastern Europe, and are generally outstripping them in access both to telecommunications and to computers. (See Table 3.)

Table 3: Access in Emerging Economies[9]

Geographical area	Telephone lines/ 100 inhabitants	Personal computers/ 100 inhabitants
Asia:		
Hong Kong	53.0	11.6
Korea (Rep.)	41.5	12.1
Malaysia	16.6	4.0
Singapore	47.9	17.2
Taiwan	43.1	8.3
Eastern Europe:		
Czech Republic	23.7	5.3
Hungary	18.5	3.9
Poland	14.8	2.9
Ukraine	16.1	0.6
Latin America:		
Argentina	16.0	2.5
Brazil	7.5	1.3
Chile	13.2	3.8
Mexico	9.6	2.6
Venezuela	11.1	1.7

As these statistics show, an enormous information gap still exists between industrialized and developing countries, and among developing countries themselves, in terms of access to both computers and the telecommunications infrastructure necessary to link them to the Internet.

INTERNET INITIATIVES FOR DEVELOPING COUNTRIES

Access to the Internet requires more than telephone lines and a computer. Internet service providers (ISPs) are required to provide connections to the network; ISPs need both technical expertise and business expertise to obtain equipment, negotiate with carriers, and serve customers. Users, in turn, have to learn how to use this information resource to support their activities, whether they are entrepreneurs looking for new markets or non-governmental organizations (NGOs) managing development projects. Several international agencies are sponsoring projects to provide Internet access in developing countries, both through support to start-up ISPs and through projects designed to enable practitioners in such fields as education, health care, and agriculture to use the Internet as a tool for development. Among these agencies are the following:

Canada's International Development Research Centre

Canada's International Development Research Centre (IDRC) operates a global networking program whose primary projects are the Acacia initiative, which addresses the information needs of sub-Saharan Africa, and the Pan Asian Networking (PAN) initiative, which is now being expanded to include other developing regions such as Latin America, the Caribbean, North Africa, and the Middle East.[10]

The Acacia initiative supports development of information and communication technologies (ICT) in Africa using a community approach. The involvement of community groups in defining Acacia's activities is designed to ensure an appropriate emphasis on (1) developing locally defined applications, services, and networks; (2) promoting innovative technical solutions to development challenges; (3) investing in technologies related to telecommunication and ICT infrastructure; and (4) supporting the development of appropriate policy environments. Another IDRC project called Unganisha (Swahili for "connectivity") has recently launched a GetWeb server to give people without direct World Wide Web access the ability to obtain Web-based information via e-mail.[11]

One of PAN's early success stories is Mongolia's MagicNet, which is discussed in detail in the next section of this chapter. Other PAN locations and projects include:

- *Bangladesh.* This project will enable Grameen Bank to establish an alternative ISP in Bangladesh, aiming to provide affordably priced Internet services to educational and research institutions, social organizations, and government agencies. Grameen Bank has received widespread acclaim for its lending to small businesses and individual entrepreneurs, particularly peasant women.

- *Laos.* Laos is one of the few countries in Asia that has no Internet access at all. This project will begin to introduce Internet-related technologies to the country through a dial-up link, an approach that will allow the ISP operator to gain technical and management experience and test the market for setting appropriate and affordable pricing of its services.[12]

- *Nepal.* The International Centre for Integrated Mountain Development (ICIMOD), situated in Kathmandu, Nepal, was established to promote the development of an economically and environmentally sound mountain ecosystem in the Hindu Kush-Himalayan region. The project will develop an Internet-based network of research and development institutions in Nepal and will be linked to the PAN network to exchange information among participating countries. The project will also provide a "drop-in" Internet site at ICIMOD in Kathmandu to promote the use of the Internet in Nepal.

- *Philippines.* This project will establish a PAN information server at the Philippine government's Department of Science and Technology to provide Philippines-based development organizations with opportunities to access and exchange information to enhance collaboration in regional programs.

USAID's Leland Initiative

The Leland Initiative (LI), sponsored by the U.S. Agency for International Development (USAID), is a five-year, $15 million U.S. government effort to extend full Internet connectivity to approximately 20 African countries in order to promote sustainable development.[13] LI (named for deceased U.S. Congressman Mickey Leland) has three major objectives: (1) to create an enabling policy environment, (2) to foster a sustainable supply of Internet services, and (3) to promote the creation of Internet user applications for sustainable development.

In December 1996, Mali became the first country to open a Leland Gateway. Ten ISPs were qualified by USAID to begin providing service in Madagascar in 1997. The Mozambique telecommunications operator also began to offer service to private ISPs under Leland in 1997. Other countries that signed bilateral policy agreements in 1996 as prerequisite to participating in LI included Rwanda, Ghana, Guinea, and the Ivory Coast. Additional countries that intend to participate are Guinea-Bissau, Benin, Eritrea, and Kenya.

Under the Leland Initiative, USAID agrees to provide policy analyses, equipment, connectivity, and training necessary to deliver robust, well-managed, and responsive Internet access. In return, the signatories agree to adopt the following "Internet-friendly" policies:

- Abandon traditional international telephone pricing for cost-based affordable tariffs;

- Allow free and open access to information on the Internet; and,

- Set aside long-standing monopoly practices in favor of private sector ISPs.

The Leland Initiative is also preparing several pilot projects to demonstrate the usefulness of Internet connectivity for agribusiness trade information centers, environmental trade links, environmental education and communication, improved local governance, and basic education.[14]

UNDP's Sustainable Development Networking Programme

The Sustainable Development Networking Programme (SDNP), sponsored by the United Nations Development Program (UNDP), is an international information-exchange operation run by independent entrepreneurs who receive equipment and seed funding from UNDP.[15] A direct result of the 1992 United Nations Conference on the Environment and Development (the "Rio Earth Summit"), the SDNP links government organizations, private-sector entities, universities, NGOs, and individuals through electronic and other networking vehicles to exchange critical information on sustainable development. SDNP operates in 24 countries; another 75 countries have expressed interest in establishing networks.

Current SDNP projects include:

- *Bolivia.* Some 180 organizations and tens of thousands of users are part of the Bolivian SDNP network. To attempt to reach all levels of civil society in a country with very limited infrastructure, the project staff uses everything from national radio announcements inviting SDNP user registration to audio cassettes sent weekly to towns without Internet access.

- *Estonia.* Estonia is making faster progress toward benefiting from the information revolution than any other country in Eastern Europe. The country already boasts more permanent

Internet connections per capita than many European Union members, and 80 percent of its schools are online. The creation of an SDNP node in Estonia has catalyzed the organization of local Estonia-related databases. This node routinely registers more than 30,000 hits per week on its Web site.

- *Nicaragua.* Nicaraguans have used the SDNP as a forum to lobby their Congress on issues related to sustainable development. This SDNP project, which has helped to update environmental laws, has become known as the source for reliable information on the environment and development.

- *Pakistan.* When the SDNP first started, there was only one other e-mail service provider in Pakistan. The SDNP publicized the importance of "being connected" in a variety of media with the result that the Pakistan SDNP now handles 2,500 nodes catering to nearly 5,000 users country-wide through its offices in four cities. In addition, eight competitive e-mail providers have entered the field in Pakistan, encouraged by the success of SDNP.[16]

The World Bank's InfoDev Project

The World Bank takes the position that information and communication technologies ". . . open up extraordinary opportunities to accelerate social and economic development, and they create a pressing reform and investment agenda both to capitalize on the new opportunities and to avoid the deterioration of international competitiveness."[17] The World Bank's InfoDev project aims to address this agenda by funding activities to assist developing countries and emerging economies in harnessing these technologies. Its strategies include leveraging funds and brokering partnerships to create a network for improved communication and information sharing.

InfoDev's main objectives are to:

- Create market-friendly environments;

- Reduce poverty and exclusion of low-income countries and social groups;

- Improve education and health;

- Promote protection of the environment and natural resources; and

- Increase the efficiency, accountability, and transparency of governments.

These objectives, which are extremely broad, probably overstate the expectations of the Bank's "informatics" professionals regarding the impact of telecommunications on development. However, they do indicate that an unwritten agenda of InfoDev may be to convince the Bank's own staff working in other sectors of the benefits of applying communications and information technologies.

InfoDev-supported activities fall into four general categories:

- Consensus-building and awareness-raising activities such as workshops, training classes, and international seminars;

- Telecommunications reform;

- Information infrastructure strategies; and

- Pilot projects.

Thus, InfoDev's activities are not limited to the Internet, nor to technology per se, but include assistance in reform of the telecommunications sector. For example, one new project will assist emerging economies to participate in the World Trade Organization's telecommunications market liberalization process. Another InfoDev project will support development of a tool kit to be used by policymakers in Africa to determine the benefits to PTTs (departments of Posts, Telephone, and Telegraph, the typical structure of the telecommunications sector in European countries and former colonies) and their countries of liberalizing value-added Internet services. The tool kit will provide a cost-benefit analysis of Internet liberalization; prepare case studies of countries which have liberalized Internet service; establish the PTTs' rationale for liberalizing this service and the expected benefits; and provide a financial model projecting specific gains and losses from an increase in Internet traffic over PTT circuits.[18]

The Soros Foundation's Internet Program

The Soros Foundation sponsors the Open Society Institute (OSI), a private foundation that promotes the development of open societies around the world.[19] Toward this goal, the institute operates and/or supports a variety of initiatives and projects in education, independent media, legal reform, and human rights. OSI is part of a network of more than two dozen autonomous nonprofit foundations and other organizations created and funded by philanthropist George Soros. The organizations exist in Central and Eastern Europe, the former Soviet Union, Haiti, South Africa, and the United States.

The OSI's Internet Program (IP) supports projects to provide Internet access as part of its strategy for fostering open civil societies. The OSI-IP program supports relatively small-scale projects (costing about $100,000) that provide access to e-mail or other Internet services. The program focuses on universities and related research institutions, secondary (and sometimes primary) schools, libraries, medical institutions, cultural centers such as museums and galleries, NGOs, independent media, environmental groups, and unaffiliated individuals who might otherwise not have access to connectivity services.

These relatively inexpensive technical projects have created tens of thousands of users in the countries they serve. The projects are usually implemented in phases, beginning with e-mail and then adding introduction of full Internet access. An important element of the program is training for telecommunications providers as well as individual users such as teachers, students, scientists, and journalists. If no other funding or service provider is available, the national foundations funded by George Soros may themselves become ISPs and seek to subsidize their connections through fee-for-service activities. The program seeks other funding sources or government entities to develop infrastructure, and fosters corporate partnerships to provide hardware and software at highly discounted prices.

From 1994 through 1996, the OSI's Internet Program committed more than $12 million to 63 projects in 28 countries, primarily in eastern Europe and the former Soviet Union. In 1995, for example, the program established e-mail connectivity to the Open Society Foundation for Albania; extended connectivity to isolated areas in Estonia using mobile radio links; purchased used computers to be installed as e-mail servers in secondary schools in Lithuania; connected three major cities to the Sofia Internet connection in Bulgaria; and gave away e-mail starter kits to universities, secondary schools, independent media, NGOs, and libraries in Georgia and Kyrgyzstan. The program provided Internet access and training for universities and/or secondary schools in Kazakstan, Poland, Moldova, Slovakia, Slovenia, and Bosnia and Herzegovina. It also provided training for the people who established the first Internet connection in Mongolia and the first bulletin board e-mail system in Tajikistan. The program committed $8.7 million for projects in 1997, and plans to expand to other developing regions.[20]

It is too soon to evaluate the impact of these pioneering initiatives; most of the projects are still in their initial stages. In many cases, these initiatives replicate the pilot-project model that has been used to introduce applications of broadcasting and telephony for development.[21] Others are exploring new approaches in which they provide not only technical but business expertise in order to build foundations for program sustainability.

THE DEVELOPMENT CONNECTION

While access remains limited in many remote and developing regions, the Internet has quickly become a valuable development tool where facilities for its use have been created. The following cases illustrate applications of the Internet for education, health care, and economic development in the Canadian Arctic, Africa, and Mongolia.

Rankin Inlet: An Arctic Window

In Rankin Inlet, a Canadian Inuit settlement on Hudson Bay "800 miles from everything," more than one in five residents has an e-mail account.[22] At night a school classroom becomes a community-access center called Igalaaq, meaning "window" in Inuktitut.

The Internet adds to the school curriculum; students exchange information with children in the Australian Outback and Hawaii and study biology using the Virtual Frog Dissection kit. But hyperlinks have the potential to strengthen indigenous culture and institutions as well. An elder teaching students to sew seal and caribou clothing uses a digital camera to record their work for posting to the Rankin Inlet Web site.[23]

Canadian Inuit have used telecommunications in the form of telephone, fax, and videoconferencing to press for land claims and greater political autonomy. Northern leaders see the Internet as a powerful communications tool to unite the isolated Inuit communities, an outlook that will help them with governance as the eastern part of the Northwest Territories becomes a separate Inuit-run territory called Nunavut ("our land") in 1999.[24]

Northerners also see the Internet's potential for economic development. Sakku Investments, the business-development arm of the local Inuit association, donates equipment and access time to Rankin Inlet's school, viewing the Internet as the electronic road system for their business development. "As far as I'm concerned," says the Sakku's CEO about Igalaaq, "it's a driver's ed school."[25]

HealthNet: Medical Links in Cyberspace

SatelLife is a Boston-based nonprofit organization that operates HealthNet, a computer network providing communications services and medical information to health-care workers in the developing world.[26] SatelLife was founded as a "broker of socially responsible connectivity between health-care workers and sources of medical information"[27] in order to provide low-cost access to medical information for health workers in countries where telecommunications facilities were either unavailable or unaffordable. Using a single low-earth-orbiting (LEO) satellite, HealthNet provides e-mail and document exchange services on a store-and-forward basis using inexpensive satellite terminals.

One of the functions of HealthNet is to provide access to medical information otherwise unavailable in underfunded medical schools in the developing world. For example, while a typical U.S. medical library subscribes to about 5,000 journals, the Nairobi University Medical School Library—regarded as a flagship center for medical literature in East Africa—receives only 20 journal titles today compared to 300 titles a decade ago because of shrinking funding and the skyrocketing cost of journals. A large district hospital in Brazzaville, Congo, served by twenty doctors, has a library consisting of a single bookshelf, while the local university hospital has only 40 outdated books and a dozen medical journals, none more recent than 1992.[28] Using HealthNet, medical staff can access BITNIS (the Batch Internet National Library of Medicine Information System) to conduct electronic searches of databases at the Washington, D.C.–based National Library of Medicine. Selected articles can then be transmitted and downloaded via satellite.

HealthNet also enables medical professionals in developing regions to share information and seek assistance. In early 1995, physicians in central Africa shared vital, up-to-the-minute information over HealthNet during the outbreak of the deadly Ebola virus. In *The Coming Plague: Newly Emerging Diseases in a World Out of Balance*,

Laurie Garrett notes: "For the first time, physicians in the developing countries could consult colleagues in neighboring nations or medical libraries and data banks to help solve puzzling cases and alert one another to disease outbreaks."[29] The Muhimbili Medical Center in Dar es Salaam, Tanzania, turned to cyberspace to help reduce high mortality rates among its pediatric burn patients. Through HealthNet, the Health Foundation in New York learned of the center's needs and responded by sending a free shipment of phenytoin, a drug that reduces pain and promotes healing of burn wounds.

SatelLife has also evolved to become an Internet gateway, providing public-health and environmental workers with an inexpensive "onramp" to the global information superhighway. The HealthNet user composes the message or research request on a computer that sends it to a national node that collects, forwards, and receives electronic messages and transmits them to the Internet four times each day. Where Internet access is now available, HealthNet's "store and forward" technology allows messages to be composed offline and stored for later delivery, avoiding the high charges incurred when conducting research or composing messages online. For physicians and researchers working in rural and isolated areas, SatelLife has built a portable ground station; it has also designed a two-way radio unit that provides users with a seamless interface to the Internet.

Mongolia: Butter to Bits

Mongolia's first Internet host was born in 1994 when its local software and networking company Datacom received a grant from Canada's IDRC to set up a low-cost dial-up Internet connection. From this modest beginning has evolved a dedicated satellite connection providing full Internet access. Users range from people in remote areas to the Prime Minister, development agencies, universities, and the new businesses that are part of the country's move from a planned to a market economy.

The collapse of the Soviet Union ended many of the subsidies and trade links that had underpinned the Mongolian economy. One of the central tasks of the new government is to reduce its spending and at the same time improve infrastructure. When the newly established Datacom first wanted to start an Internet service, lack of funds was the major stumbling block. The PAN program chose Mongolia as its first pilot site not only because Mongolia desperately needed information to help with the transition to a market economy, but also because the country had technical expertise available in Datacom.

Problems included unreliable telephone lines, telephone exchanges based on non-standard and outdated Russian technology, erratic power, and few computers. However, even at this early stage, Datacom had already created its own messaging system, adapted from Russian software, which was robust enough to cope with the conditions. In late 1994, Datacom installed a dial-up gateway system to connect its domestic system to the Internet. The network was named MagicNet (for Mongolia Access to Global Information and Communications).[30]

At first, data were transmitted once a day, then twice daily as traffic grew. Datacom's goal was to have a permanent Internet connection. The most economical and feasible connection turned out to be via satellite; MagicNet now uses a 128 kbps leased satellite circuit to SprintLink via PanAmSat 2. The U.S. National Science Foundation (NSF) agreed to pay the leasing costs if Datacom would give Mongolia's educational institutions free Internet access. A government loan, known locally as the "butter fund," was established through a U.S. Department of Agriculture donation of surplus butter. The Mongolian government sold the butter on the domestic market, thus creating a fund for loans and grants that could be used for special projects.

The Asian Development Bank has recently injected funds into the local PTT to upgrade and extend the national network outside the capital, Ulaan Bataar. One of the first improvements will be a high-capacity microwave link to two major centers, Erdenet and Darhan. Datacom itself is involved in the installation of a private VSAT (very small aperture [satellite] terminal) network that is already being deployed in 20 provincial areas. The project is financed by a Mongolian oil import corporation, but there is also agreement for public Internet e-mail access, which will be managed by Datacom.

Mongolia's education sector is also receiving assistance from NSF to improve connections to the universities through grants for radio modems. In a similar arrangement, the International Science Foundation (ISF), established by financier George Soros to support scientific projects in countries aligned with the former Soviet Union, is giving grants to another six organizations in Mongolia to provide radio modem links to Datacom's network. The ISF is also funding a public Internet center to be located within the Ulaan Bataar public library.[31]

These projects provide snapshots of how people in the developing world are getting access to the Internet, and how creatively children, teachers, health-care professionals and entrepreneurs are using this new means of finding and sharing information to foster their own development.

GLOBAL ACCESS TO THE INTERNET: TOWARD GII

The phenomenal growth and visibility of the Internet as an information resource, communications tool, and electronic marketplace have focused attention on the need to bring the Internet and other forms of electronic communications within reach of people around the world. In 1993, the newly elected Clinton administration called for investment in a national "information infrastructure" to bring the benefits of "advanced services," and particularly the Internet, to Americans not only in the workplace, but in schools, libraries, health-care centers, and individual households.[32]

Vice President Al Gore elaborated on this theme at the International Telecommunication Union's 1994 Development Conference in Buenos Aires, calling for a Global Information Infrastructure (GII) to extend access to these new technologies and services to people throughout the developing world.[33] Policymakers in various fora such as the European Union, the G7,[34] and APEC[35] have taken up the call, with support for pilot projects and strategies to accelerate investment in telecommunications networks.

Beyond Technology

Despite their development goals, these GII initiatives are often technology-driven, which is not overly surprising as their major instigators are generally technical ministries, telecommunications operators, and equipment suppliers. Applications projects too often appear as afterthoughts, planned to take advantage of available facilities rather than to meet the needs of—for example—educators, health-care providers, or NGOs. These "information highway" initiatives assume that converging technologies will result in information services with both social and economic benefits. Yet this assumption needs to be carefully examined.

Each new communication technology has been heralded at its advent as a potential source of numerous benefits. Satellites and cable television were to provide courses taught by the best instructors to students in schools, homes, and workplaces. Videoconferencing was to largely eliminate business travel. Telemedicine was to replace referral of patients to specialists. Computers were to replace traditional teaching with more personalized and interactive instruction.

To some extent all of these prophesies have been fulfilled, yet the potential of the technologies is far from fully realized. In many cases, institutional changes and incentives to innovate must appear before these technologies have much effect. In North America, the most remarkable ongoing change is in these incentives to innovate rather than in the technologies themselves. As school districts face shrinking budgets and new curricular requirements, as spiraling health-care budgets are targeted by governments and insurance companies, and as businesses realize that people must "work smarter" to compete in a global economy, they find new and compelling reasons to turn to already-existing telecommunications and information technologies.

Thus, investment in technology alone will not likely result in major social benefits. Policymakers appear aware that public-sector stimulus is needed to foster new educational and social service applications. Yet seed money for pilot projects may not ensure long-term implementation. If the services are perceived as "frills" that only divert energy and resources from higher priorities, or if there is no budget allocation to buy computers or pay monthly usage charges, the first flurry of Internet activity will produce few benefits.

The Need for Structural Reform

As investment in telecommunications infrastructure increases, the gap between information haves and have-nots may well have more to do with price and choice than technology. Countries that continue to favor telecommunications monopolies, or seek to control access to information, may limit user access even where technology is available. In most of Europe, for example, access to the Internet is much more expensive than it is in North America. As *Internet World* notes, "Digital Europe has many medieval features: road tolls and extortion-like taxes, witch hunts, an oppressed citizenry, and powers-that-be in feudal towers."[36] And access is even more expensive in many developing countries.

Some programs such as the Leland Initiative and InfoDev emphasize the importance of opening telecommunications markets, and provide policy assistance in planning and implementing reform. Open entry for value-added services will spur the formation of ISPs. Competition in national and international services will also be necessary to lower the prices of Internet usage. Users' response to unaffordable prices is increasingly to bypass local networks. Today in most developing countries, people with telephones can access callback services to make international calls at a fraction of the price charged by their own international operators.

Many governments remain highly skeptical about opening the public networks to competition, especially where the government is still the telecommunications operator.[37] For example, these public telecommunications operators (PTOs) claim that callback is siphoning off revenues that they need to expand their networks, which would in turn create more jobs. However, the equation is not so simple. For example, the operator of an ISP from Guinea-Bissau pointed out that without callback, he would not be in business. He needs a relatively inexpensive international connection to the Internet in order to provide affordable Internet access for his customers. By using bypass, he is creating new jobs in value-added services as an Internet provider, as well as providing an important information resource for economic development of the country.[38]

HealthNet, described above, began to use a LEO satellite for store-and-forward text communications in Africa in 1988. It took the SatelLife organization several years to get licenses to operate this simple low-capacity service in some African countries. Today, domestic and international geostationary satellites provide Internet connections in isolated and poorly served regions. The Igalaaq project described above connects children in the Canadian Arctic to the Internet via Canada's Anik satellite. Across North America in Alaska, Internet service is also reaching Alaskan villages via satellite.[39] GCI, an Alaskan telecommunications carrier, reports that villagers who pressed for telephone and television service twenty years ago are now asking for Internet access.[40] Mongolia's MagicNet leases circuits on PanAmSat to reach SprintLink.[41] PanAmSat recently announced that it was going to provide Internet service for an ISP in Togo.[42]

New satellite technologies may provide additional pathways to the Internet. Hughes' DirecPC uses telephone lines to reach the Internet, but transmits requested information back to the user over a high-capacity satellite link. Multiple-satellite LEO systems will provide real-time interaction, but generally at very low bandwidth. An exception is the proposed Teledesic system that promises bandwidth on demand via satellite. New generations of geostationary satellites will also offer high capacity links to the Internet. However, operators of these systems will need permission from national governments to offer these services.

OPENING THE DOOR

An unspoken concern among governments of many developing countries is the potential negative impact of the Internet's foreign content because of its ability to link individuals and organizations across the country and the world. Many policy makers appear to share Deng Xiaoping's ambivalence about opening China's doors to the world: "When the door opens, some flies are bound to come in."[43] China and Singapore are among countries blocking access to controversial Internet sites and tracking Internet users. Singapore has also decided to apply the standards of broadcasting content to the Internet, holding Internet access providers accountable for information on their networks.

Clever users will inevitably find means to bypass these roadblocks, as shown by dissidents' use of facsimile and electronic mail during the Tiananmen Square uprising in China, the proliferation of satellite antennae in countries where they are officially banned, and the widespread availability of supposedly illegal callback services that undercut international tariffs. Yet these strategies are likely to be limited to an elite few with the technical expertise or political connections to end-run the regulations.

Ironically, some developing-country policy makers are reluctant to acknowledge that the inevitable result of investing in information infrastructure is to increase access to information. As Internet pioneers in developing countries are demonstrating, it will be the sharing and utilization of information, not the mere existence of networks, that will contribute to their future development.

ENDNOTES

1. Quoted online at http://www3.undp.org.
2. For in-depth introductions to the development of the Internet, see Anthony M. Rutkowski, "The Internet: An Abstraction in Chaos" (1–22), and Hal R. Varian, "Economic Issues Facing the Internet" (23–46), both in *The Internet as Paradigm* (Institute for Information Studies, 1997).
3. See Heather E. Hudson, "Universal Service in the Information Age," *Telecommunications Policy*, November 1994, 658–67.
4. These income categories, which were established using World Bank methodology, are based on per-capita Gross National Product (GNP):

High income:	GNP $US 8,956 or more (per capita)
Upper-middle income:	GNP $US 2,896–8,955
Lower-middle income:	GNP $US 726–2,895
Low income:	GNP $US 725 or less

5. Source: International Telecommunication Union (ITU), *World Telecommunication Development Report 1996–97* (Geneva: ITU, 1997).
6. Source: http://www.nw.com/zone/host-count-history.
7. Source: http://www.genmagic.com/Internet/Trends.
8. Source: ITU, *World Telecommunication Development Report 1996–97*.
9. Source: Ibid.
10. See Canada's International Development Research Centre (IDRC) online at http://www.idrc.org; see the IDRC's Acacia initiative online at http://www.idrc.ca/acacia/ and its Pan Asian Networking (PAN) initiative online at http://www.idrc.ca/institution/e1_panntwk.html.
11. See information about the Unganisha GetWeb server online at http://www.idrc.ca/unganisha/activities.html.
12. See PAN's Laos project online at http://www.PanAsia.org.sg/la01i000.htm.
13. See USAID's Leland Initiative online at http://www.info.usaid.gov/regions/afr/leland.
14. USAID Bureau for Africa, Office of Sustainable Development, "Leland Initiative: Africa GII Gateway Project." Available online at http://www.info.usaid.gov/regions/afr/leland.
15. See the United Nations Development Program online at http://www.undp.org.
16. Chuck Lankester and Richard Labelle, "The Sustainable Development Networking Programme (SDNP): 1992–1997" (New York: UNDP, June 1997). Paper originally presented at the Global Knowledge Conference, Toronto, 22–26 June 1997.
17. Source: InfoDev, online at http://www.worldbank.org/html/fpd/infodev/infodev.html.
18. Ibid.
19. See the Soros Foundation online at http://www.soros.org; see the Open Society Institute (OSI) and its Internet Program online at http://www.soros.org/osiny.html.
20. Source: http://www.soros.org/osiny.html.
21. See Heather E. Hudson, *Global Connections: International Telecommunications Infrastructure and Policy* (New York: Van Nostrand Reinhold, 1997).

22. See Ken MacQueen, "Surfing the World from the Frozen North," *Ottawa Citizen*, 23 February 1997; available online at http://www.Ottawacitizen.com/national.

23. See the Rankin Inlet Web site at http://www.arctic.ca/LUS.

24. Indigenous peoples who call themselves the "fourth world" are also using the Internet to link aboriginal organizations throughout the world to share concerns and organize to press for human rights and environmental issues.

25. MacQueen, "Surfing the World from the Frozen North."

26. See HealthNet online at http://www.healthnet.org.

27. Quoted at http://www.healthnet.org.

28. Source: http://www.healthnet.org.

29. Laurie Garrett, *The Coming Plague: Newly Emerging Diseases in a World Out of Balance* (New York: Farrar, Straus, and Giroux, 1994), quoted at http://www.healthnet.org.

30. See MagicNet at http://www.magicnet.mn.

31. Source: http://www.PanAsia.org.sg/mn01i000.htm.

32. Quoted in Information Infrastructure Task Force, *The National Information Infrastructure: Agenda for Action* (Washington, D.C.: U.S. Department of Commerce, September 1993).

33. Quoted in U.S. Department of Commerce, *The Global Information Infrastructure: Agenda for Cooperation* (Washington, D.C.: Department of Commerce, 1995).

34. The "G7" is a grouping of the world's major industrialized economies: Canada, France, Germany, Italy, Japan, the United Kingdom, and the United States.

35. APEC (the Asia Pacific Economic Conference) is an association of Asian and Pacific nations.

36. Brent Gregston, "Power and Privilege," *Internet World*, November 1995, 96.

37. See Heather E. Hudson, "Privatization and Liberalization in the Developing World: The Need for New Policies and Strategies," in *Privatization and Competition in Telecommunications: International Developments*, ed. Daniel J. Ryan (Westport, Conn.: Praeger, 1997).

38. Personal communication, July 1997.

39. For information about Internet connectivity in Alaska, see Beverly Hunter, "Learning in an Internetworked World," in *The Internet as Paradigm* (Institute for Information Studies, 1997), 107–111.

40. Richard Dowling, General Communications, Inc., personal communication, January 1997.

41. Source: http://www. magicnet.mn.

42. Source: http://www.panamsat.com/ctext.htm.

43. Steven Schwankert, "Dragons at the Gates," *Internet World*, November 1995, 112.

AUTHORS

INTRODUCTION
Arthur A. Bushkin

Arthur A. Bushkin, an expert in the computer, communications, information, and Internet and online services industries, is President and Chief Operating Officer of Pace Financial Network, L.L.C., a new business that uses direct marketing and the World Wide Web to provide an array of high-quality, low-cost financial products and services to members, customers, supporters, and affiliates of a variety of targeted affinity groups. He is also President of Galway Partners, L.L.C., an investment and merchant bank that provides financial and advisory services and specializes in creating new companies and new business opportunities. Mr. Bushkin studied computer science at MIT, where he received his S.B., S.M., and E.E. degrees.

SOVEREIGNTY IN THE NETWORKED WORLD
Michael R. Nelson

Michael R. Nelson is Director for Technology Policy in the Office of Plans and Policy at the U.S. Federal Communications Commission (FCC). In this position, Dr. Nelson focuses on the interface between technology and policy making, working on such issues as improving the reliability and security of the nation's telecommunication networks, understanding the convergence of communications and computing, and using FCC policies to spur development and deployment of new technologies. Prior to joining the FCC, Dr. Nelson was Special Assistant for Information Technology at the White House Office of Science and Technology Policy, where he worked on a range of issues relating to the Global Information Infrastructure, including telecommunications policy, information technology, electronic commerce, and information policy. Dr. Nelson received a B.S. in geology from Caltech and a Ph.D. in geophysics from MIT.

THE NEW "CIVIC VIRTUE" OF THE INTERNET
David R. Johnson and David G. Post

David R. Johnson currently serves as Director of the Aspen Institute Internet Policy Project. He is also Co-Director of the Cyberspace Law Institute. A graduate of Yale College, Mr. Johnson studied at University College, Oxford, and received his law degree from Yale Law School in 1972. He clerked for Judge Malcolm R. Wilkey of the United States Court of Appeals for the District of Columbia. He then joined the Washington, D.C., law firm of Wilmer, Cutler & Pickering, and was admitted to the partnership in 1980. In recent years, he has practiced computer law, focusing on software and systems contracting, electronic publishing, and privacy issues. He helped write the Electronic Communications Privacy Act and has counseled major online system providers.

David G. Post is an Associate Professor of Law at Temple University Law School in Philadelphia. He is also Co-Founder and Co-Director of the Cyberspace Law Institute. Mr. Post received his law degree from Georgetown Law Center in 1986. After clerking with then-Judge Ruth Bader Ginsburg on the D.C. Circuit Court of Appeals, he joined the Washington, D.C., law firm of Wilmer, Cutler & Pickering, practicing in the areas of intellectual property law and high-technology commercial transactions. He then clerked again for Justice Ginsburg during her first term at the Supreme Court of the United States, after which he joined the faculty at the Georgetown Law Center, where he taught constitutional and copyright law as well as the "law of cyberspace." He also writes a monthly column on law and technology for the *American Lawyer.*

THE INTERNET AND COMMUNITY
Jeffrey Abramson

Jeffrey Abramson holds the Louis Stulberg Chair of Law and Politics at Brandeis University, where he teaches law and political thought. He has written widely on law, the media, and political theory. His latest book, *We, The Jury: The Jury System and the Ideal of Democracy*, was a finalist for the Los Angeles Times Book Prize and was awarded a Citation of Merit by the American Bar Association. His previous book, *The Electronic Commonwealth: The Impact of New Media Technologies on Democratic Values*, was a finalist for the National Association of Broadcasters' Prize for Best Books of 1988. A graduate of Amherst College, Professor Abramson received his J.D. from Harvard Law School and his Ph.D. in political science from Harvard University.

WILL THE INTERNET TRANSFORM HIGHER EDUCATION?
Walter S. Baer

Walter S. Baer is Senior Policy Analyst in RAND's Science and Technology Division, where he directs research on interactive media, telecommunications, and information infrastructure developments. Previously, as Deputy Vice President of RAND's Domestic Research Division, Dr. Baer led efforts to establish the Critical Technologies Institute, which provides analytic support on technology policy issues for the White House Office of Science and Technology Policy. He has published widely in the fields of media, communications, information technology, energy, and science and technology policy; his book *Cable Television: A Handbook for Decisionmaking* received a Preceptor Award from the Broadcast Industry Conference. Dr. Baer holds a B.S. from the California Institute of Technology and a Ph.D. in physics from the University of Wisconsin.

THE INTERNET AND ELECTRONIC COMMERCE:
A TALE OF THREE CITIES
Elliot Maxwell

Elliot Maxwell is Deputy Chief of the Office of Plans and Policy, U.S. Federal Communications Commission (FCC), which is deeply involved in implementing the Telecommunication Act of 1996 and is locus for the Commission's analysis of the Internet's impact on telecommunications policy. Previously, he was Director of International Trade Policy at the U.S. Department of Commerce, leading efforts to ensure that U.S. international policies serve to promote the development and diffusion of U.S. technology and increase U.S. access to foreign technology. Mr. Maxwell spent nearly a decade working for Pacific Telesis Group as Assistant Vice President for Corporate Strategy, supervising a multidisciplinary staff charged with integrating business, technology, and public-policy planning. He received a B.A. from Brown University and a law degree from Yale University. He is a recipient of a Fulbright Fellowship for study in Japan.

DEVELOPMENT AND THE GLOBALIZATION
OF CYBERSPACE
Heather E. Hudson

Heather E. Hudson is Director of the Telecommunications Management and Policy Program in the McLaren School of Business at the University of San Francisco. An expert on telecommunications applications and domestic and international policy issues such as universal service, information infrastructure, and telecommunications planning for socioeconomic development, Dr. Hudson is author of *Global Connections: International Telecommunications Infrastructure and Policy* (1997), *Satellites: Their Development and Impact* (1990), and *When Telephones Reach the Village* (1984). She is co-author of *Electronic Byways: State Policies for Rural Development through Telecommunications* (1992) and *Rural America in the Information Age* (1989). Dr. Hudson received her B.A. in English from the University of British Columbia, her M.A. and Ph.D. in Communication Research from Stanford University, and her J.D. from the University of Texas at Austin.

ACKNOWLEDGMENTS

A critique session for the essays commissioned for the *Annual Review* was held at The Aspen Institute in Queenstown, Maryland, June 19–20, 1997. A select group of reviewers knowledgeable in the field of information technology, its problems and potentials, met with the authors and representatives of the Institute for Information Studies to provide a diversity of voices, views, and insights aimed at informing the final editing of the text. A list of participants follows.

Additional support in the editing and production of the *Annual Review* was provided by Elizabeth A. Macom, independent editor; Barbara Bimonte, program associate, the Institute for Information Studies and the Communications and Society Program, The Aspen Institute; Carolyn Uhl, graphic production, The Aspen Institute; and Sylvia Pear, publications manager, The Aspen Institute.

Gary Arlen
Arlen Communications Inc.
Bethesda, Maryland

Andrew Blau
Director, Communications
    Policy & Practice
The Benton Foundation
Washington, D.C.

Marjory S. Blumenthal
Executive Director
Computer Science &
    Telecommunications Board
National Research Council
Washington, D.C.

Ordering Information

The Emerging Internet is the ninth volume of the *Annual Review* of the Institute for Information Studies. Individual copies are available for $12.00. Limited numbers of earlier volumes are also available. To order, contact:

Barbara Bimonte
The Institute for Information Studies
P. O. Box 222
Queenstown, MD 21658
Voice: 410-820-5375
Fax: 410-820-5460
E-mail: bimonte@aspeninst.org

To access information and abstracts for this and earlier volumes, visit our home page on the World Wide Web at http://www.aspeninst.org/dir/polpro/CSP/IIS.html:

- *The Emerging Internet* — 1998

- *The Internet as Paradigm* — 1997

- *The Emerging World of Wireless Communications* — 1996

- *Crossroads on the Information Highway: Convergence and Diversity in Communications Technologies* — 1995

- *The Knowledge Economy: The Nature of Information in the 21st Century* — 1993–1994

- *A National Information Network: Changing Our Lives in the 21st Century* — 1992

- *Universal Telephone Service: Ready for the 21st Century?* — 1991

- *The Annual Review* — 1990

- *Paradigms Revised: The Annual Review of Communications and Society* — 1989